GUIDEPOSTS

THE HIDDEN HAND OF GOD

ALL GOD'S CHILDREN

THE HIDDEN HAND OF GOD

ALL GOD'S CHILDREN

Surely there are in everyone's life certain connections, twists and
turns which pass awhile under the category of Chance, but at
the last, well examined, prove to be the very hand of God.
—Sir Thomas Browne

Guideposts®
CARMEL, NEW YORK 10512

www.guidepostsbooks.com

Acknowledgments

Every attempt has been made to credit the sources of copyrighted material used in this book. If any such acknowledgment has been inadvertently omitted or miscredited, receipt of such information would be appreciated.

All material that originally appeared in *Angels on Earth* and *Guideposts* magazine is reprinted with permission. Copyright © 1979, 1989, 1996, 1997, 1998 and 2000 by Guideposts, Carmel, New York 10512. All rights reserved.

All Scripture quotations, unless otherwise noted, are taken from *The Holy Bible, New International Version*. Copyright 1973, 1978, 1984 International Bible Society. Used by permission of Zondervan Bible Publishers.

Scripture quotations marked (KJV) are taken from *The King James Version of the Bible*.

"Adopting a Dream" by Kathryn Lay is reprinted by permission of Kathryn Lay. Copyright © 1997 by Kathryn Lay.

"Always Near," "The Last Christmas Gift" and "The True Thanksgiving" by Joan Wester Anderson appeared in *Where Miracles Happen: True Stories of Heavenly Encounters* by Joan Wester Anderson. Copyright © 1994 by Joan Wester Anderson. Published by Brett Books, Inc. Reprinted by permission.

"An Angel Provided Money for the Overdue Bill" by Brad Steiger and Sherry Hansen Steiger appeared in *Angels Around the World*. Copyright © 1996 by Brad Steiger and Sherry Hansen Steiger. Published by the Ballantine Publishing Group, a division of Random House, Inc.

"Anna's Cure" by Rebekah Montgomery appeared in *Ordinary Miracles*. Copyright © 2000 by Rebekah Montgomery. Published by Promise Press, an imprint of Barbour Publishing, Inc.

"Another Miracle Baby" and "Answered Prayer" by Jodie Berndt appeared in *Celebration of Miracles*. Copyright © 1995 by Jodie Berndt. Published by Thomas Nelson Publishers.

"The Baby from Heaven" and "Pray, Mama, Pray!" by Kelsey Tyler appeared in *Heaven's Littlest Angels*. Copyright © 1997 by Karen Kingsbury. Published by the Berkley Publishing Group.

"Christmas Loaves and Fishes" by Raynier Maharaj appeared in *Christmas Miracles*, compiled and edited by Jamie C. Miller, Laura Lewis, and Jennifer Basye Sander. Copyright © 1997 by Jamie C. Miller, Laura Lewis, and Jennifer Basye Sander. Published by William Morrow and Company, Inc., a division of HarperCollins, Inc.

"The Day Healing Began" by Marilyn K. Strube is reprinted by permission of the author. Copyright © 1999 by Marilyn K. Strube.

"Disappearing Roof" by John Fitch appeared in *Expect Miracles* by Mary Ellen. Copyright © 1999 by Mary Ellen Angelscribe. Used by permission of Conari Press.

(*Continued on page 175*)

THE HIDDEN HAND OF GOD

ALL GOD'S CHILDREN

Introduction. . . ix

Chapter 1 God Answers My Prayers. . . 1

Another Miracle Baby *by Jodie Berndt*, 3
Saving Quacks *by Patti Maguire Armstrong*, 9
"Pray, Mama, Pray!" *by Kelsey Tyler*, 13
Answered Prayer *by Jodie Berndt*, 26
Lost and Found *by Ann Spangler*, 31

Chapter 2 God Keeps Me Safe. . . 33

Always Near *by Joan Wester Anderson*, 35
The "Good Fear" Angel *by Charlie W. Shedd*, 38
The Snakebite *by Debbie Durrance*, 40
The Last Christmas Gift *by Joan Wester Anderson*, 48
A Pope's Blessing *by Marie Foley Nielsen*, 51
Disappearing Roof *by John Fitch*, 54
Steering Clear *by Joan Wester Anderson*, 56
When We Fall, It's to a Place of Grace *by David Waters*, 59

Chapter 3 God Supplies My Needs. . . 64

Psalm 81:10 *by Candy Chand*, 66
Our Mysterious Benefactor *by Jan Jakeman*, 69

An Angel Provided Money for the Overdue Bill
by Brad Steiger and Sherry Hansen Steiger, 73
"Mijo, the Lord Will Provide" *by Isaac J. Canales*, 76
Christmas Loaves and Fishes *by Raynier Maharaj*, 80

Chapter 4 God Heals My Hurts. . . 83
The Gardener *by Donna McDonnall*, 85
"What Did She Put on My Sister's Face?" *by Jackie, as told to Charlie W. Shedd*, 93
Anna's Cure *by Rebekah Montgomery*, 96
The Healing *by Sandy Jones*, 103
The True Thanksgiving *by Joan Wester Anderson*, 106

Chapter 5 God Is Generous with His Miracles. . . 110
For Love of Logan *by Joan Wester Anderson*, 112
The Miracle Baby *by John Holmstrom*, 122
The Baby from Heaven *by Kelsey Tyler*, 130
Adopting a Dream *by Kathryn Lay*, 140
The Earthmover *by Les Brown*, 144

Chapter 6 God's Lessons Last a Lifetime. . . 148
Cup Full of Water *by Clara Wallace Nail*, 150
Picture Perfect *by Hope Gardner*, 153
The Day Healing Began *by Marilyn K. Strube*, 157
Heart Sounds *by Tim Madigan*, 163
Just Make Room *by Marion Bond West*, 170

People were bringing little children to Jesus to have him touch them, but the disciples rebuked them. When Jesus saw this, he was indignant. He said to them, "Let the little children come to me, and do not hinder them, for the kingdom of God belongs to such as these. I tell you the truth, anyone who will not receive the kingdom of God like a little child will never enter it." And he took the children in his arms, put his hands on them and blessed them (Mark 10:13–16).

Children get it. They just get it. To adults, the world is complex: Love is difficult, life is dangerous, and God is just a mystery. But children know better. Jesus enjoyed children because they approach life with open hands and hearts. Unlike adults, who generally think in terms of negotiation and earning power, kids understand that they are dependent on the goodness and love of others—their parents, their teachers, their grandparents, brothers and sisters, uncles and aunts. Children are happy to receive—especially when it's a gift like love.

Throughout the Scripture the writers describe God's compassion and tenderness as the love of a parent toward a child. The gods of the gentiles were made of stone and wood, vile and angry gods whose worship demanded appeasement, sometimes even the sacrifice of children. The living God of Israel, on the other hand, was a personal God, not a piece of stone or carved tree.

He sought a relationship with His people, a chance to listen and be heard, to know and be known—a chance to love and be loved. It was this relationship that God jealously sought and protected, and it was this relationship that Jesus reflected in His life and described in His teaching. Jesus talks openly and frequently of His Father, revealing the loving and vital relationship that He encouraged His followers to find for themselves. And how better illustrate God's love than to use a parent's love for a child? So Jesus see welcome children when others would have pushed them aside.

In truth, we are all children when we approach God. We come to Him helpless and empty-handed, dependent and needy. We come with all the vulnerabilities of children, seeking comfort, solace and love. What God offers us is an intimacy afforded a beloved child, allowing us to know Him as *Abba*, or Father. In his book *Abba's Child*, Brennan Manning marvels:

> The average American child begins to speak at the age of eighteen months. Invariably, the first word formulated is "Da, da, dad, daddy." At the same age level, a Jewish child in first-century Palestine would say in Aramaic, "Ab, Ab, Abba, Abba." The revolutionary revelation of Jesus lies precisely in this: the infinitely holy God, in whose presence Moses had to remove his

shoes, the God from whose fingertips universes fall, the God beside whose beauty the Grand Canyon is only a shadow, the God beside whose power the nuclear bomb is nothing, may be addressed with the same intimacy, familiarity, tenderness and reverence as an eighteen-month-old child resting on his father's lap.

Jesus tried to help us understand God's great love for us: "Which of you, if his son asks for bread, will give him a stone? Or if he asks for a fish, will give him a snake? If you, then, though you are evil, know how to give good gifts to your children, how much more will your Father in heaven give good gifts to those who ask him!" (Matthew 7:9–11). Like a father who gives good things to his children, God gives us good things because He is a good and faithful God.

A child eagerly asks for help and expects God's miraculous response. A child will approach Him with an open and trusting heart, expecting good things. How often the miracles of God feature children in starring roles. God answers their prayers and heals their hurts, He provides for their needs and sends His angels to protect them. The stories that follow celebrate God's faithfulness to His children, whatever their age. May we never forget how to be open and trusting with God, always remembering the lesson of children, what they know about God, and what they can teach us.

My heart is not proud, O LORD,
my eyes are not haughty;
I do not concern myself with great matters
or things too wonderful for me.
But I have stilled and quieted my soul;
like a weaned child with its mother,
like a weaned child is my soul within me.
O Israel, put your hope in the LORD
both now and forevermore.

—Psalm 131:1–3

Chapter 1   God Answers My Prayers

If ever a child was wanted, it was Samuel. His mother Hannah struggled for years with infertility. Year after year, she prayed for children, to no avail. Her husband loved her dearly, but for her nothing less than children would do. Finally, she reached the end of her rope during their annual visit to Jerusalem. Hannah went to the temple to pray and plead her case to God. She promised Him that if He gave her a son, she would give him into God's service. She wanted a son, and she was willing to bargain.

The priest Eli found her weeping with her lips moving in prayer, and accused her of being drunk. He tried to send her home, but Hannah protested. "Not so, my lord . . . I am a woman who is deeply troubled. I have not been drinking wine or beer; I was pouring out my soul to the LORD. Do not take your servant for a wicked woman; I have been praying here out of my great anguish and grief" (1 Samuel 1:15–16). To which Eli replied, "Go in peace, and may the God of Israel grant you what you have asked of him" (1 Samuel 1:17).

Well, we all know what happened. Hannah did have a son, and true to her word, once the boy was weaned—maybe at three or four years old—she returned to temple and to the priest Eli, and in her arms was her son. She said to the priest, "As surely as you live, my lord, I am the woman who stood here beside you praying to the LORD

I prayed for this child, and the LORD has granted me what I asked of him. So now I give him to the LORD" (1 Samuel 1:26–28).

We read that Hannah and her husband returned to the temple every year with a robe for their firstborn, and God blessed them with three more sons and two daughters. But it was this first son Samuel who would forever witness to God's faithfulness. The child Samuel knew firsthand that God answered prayer because he himself was an answer to prayer. His very name proclaimed it: Hannah named him Samuel, for she said it meant "Because I asked the LORD for him" (1 Samuel 1:20).

> "My heart rejoices in the LORD;
> in the LORD my horn is lifted high.
> My mouth boasts over my enemies,
> for I delight in your deliverance.
> There is no one holy like the LORD;
> there is no one besides you;
> there is no Rock like our God."
>
> —1 Samuel 2:1–2

ANOTHER MIRACLE BABY

JODIE BERNDT

Lara Woods looked forward to motherhood, and her job as a pediatric nurse only strengthened her love for children. Working in the pediatric intensive care unit at Vanderbilt University Hospital—where her husband Joe was a plastic surgery fellow—Lara saw infants and children struggle against disease, deformation, and even death. Despite the tragedy she often faced, Lara loved her profession. Nothing, she thought, could be better than helping a child triumph over sickness and despair.

When Lara learned she was pregnant, she and Joe could scarcely contain their joy. They heard the baby's heartbeat, and their anticipation grew. They could hardly wait for the ultrasound, a routine examination; it would allow them to "see" their eighteen-week-old baby as he or she kicked and moved in Lara's uterus.

The day finally came, and as the technician manipulated the ultrasound equipment, Joe and Lara watched in fascination. They had seen ultrasound pictures before, but these images were special. They were watching their very own child—and already they were in love.

"Oh, my gosh," the technician said, interrupting the couple's reverie. "Wait a minute . . . um, excuse me."

With no more explanation, the technician left the room. Time dragged on, and Lara and Joe began to wonder. Was this standard procedure? Vanderbilt was a teaching hospital—and therefore notoriously slow—but surely they could not be expected to wait much longer. Finally the door opened, and a radiologist introduced himself.

The radiologist read the ultrasound and without elaboration said, "You need to see your doctor right now."

Numb and confused, Lara and Joe made their way to the obstetrician's office. "What's going on?" Lara pleaded to Joe. He did not know; never before had either of them experienced such a sense of frustration. *Was this how all patients felt?* they wondered. *Like victims?*

Lara's doctor was gentle and kind, yet nothing could take the sting out of his words. "There is a problem with your baby," he said.

With that, Lara's pent-up emotions broke loose, and she began to sob. Dimly, she heard the doctor explain the situation. A right choroid plexus cyst about half the size of a dime had developed in the baby's brain. As she struggled to comprehend what that meant, Lara realized the doctor was still speaking.

"This problem is extremely rare," he said. "In fact, I've never actually seen this before now. There are people at this hospital who will advise you to abort the pregnancy, but I believe there is a chance—however remote—that things may be all right.

end this pregnancy," she said. "You need to seriously consider having an abortion—my duty as an obstetrician is to tell you that you need to do it *now*."

Lara thanked the woman for her professional advice and ended the discussion. She knew she could not abort her baby. Moreover, she could not escape the strange sensation that, even as she carried her unborn child, God was somehow carrying her, bearing her along in His arms.

When the follow-up ultrasound appointment arrived, Joe excused himself from surgery and joined Lara in the technician's office. The technician was not the same fellow who had discovered the cyst, but he had read the charts and his look was not encouraging. Lara held her breath as she waited for his report. Had the cyst grown? Was it worse than she and Joe had anticipated?

The technician moved his instruments and began muttering to himself. "I do not believe this," he said over and over again.

Lara's heart was in her throat and she began to weep. "What" she demanded. "Is it worse? *Is the baby dead?*"

"No," the technician replied. "The cyst is not there. I mean, I can't find it. I need someone else to come and look."

The radiologist was summoned, and as he reviewed the pictures he shook his head. "This is very unusual," he said. "These cysts rarely go away."

The radiologist maintained his composure, but the technician could not hold back. "This is wonderful!" he exclaimed, and then he began to cry. "I mean, this is so *weird*!"

"Well, this baby has been prayed for," Lara said, through her own grateful tears. She turned to Joe, who had a look of wonder on his face. After four years of medical school and six years in residency, he understood something that none of his schooling had taught him: God is greater than anything science and medicine have to offer. His power, unlike a surgeon's, knows no limits.

Ten weeks later Lara gave birth to a baby girl named Emily. It was the middle of the night, and the pediatrician who examined Emily had tears in his eyes.

"You have a perfectly normal baby girl," he said. "I heard about this baby from a friend who is in your small group, and I have been praying for you for the past ten weeks. This is truly a miracle baby."

SAVING QUACKS

PATTI MAGUIRE ARMSTRONG

It was the day my eleven-year-old son Luke had long anticipated. On a sunny August afternoon the ducks he had been begging for had finally arrived.

We had recently moved to the country, and Luke was impatient with the pace at which we were acquiring animals. Two dogs, two cats, a bunny and an ever-growing frog population just weren't enough. So we brought home a dozen ducklings. Luke put them in the pen he had constructed and filled a plastic wading pool picked up at a rummage sale. The twelve fuzzy peepers immediately got to work swimming, waddling and gobbling up the grasshoppers that had invaded North Dakota in waves that summer.

Actually, it was those pesky garden-munching grasshoppers that had hastened the ducks' arrival. My husband Mark announced that his garden had had enough abuse. When he learned ducks were grasshopper-eating machines he was more than glad to get a dozen.

The ducks immediately became Luke's primary responsibility, but the rest of the family took an interest too. Aaron, age thirteen, named two of them McCoy and Kirk. Tyler, eight, named his favorites Sunshine and Stripes. Jacob, six, dubbed one Web. Mary, two, and Teresa, three months, were content just to watch the little birds. Luke christened the rest Midnight, Donald, Scrooge, Lightning, Captain Picard, Gizmo and his favorite—Quacks.

Quacks was the runt. He sported a soft yellow bib on his otherwise light-brown body. Right from the start Luke discovered Quacks enjoyed being held and would nuzzle up to him.

Soon afterward, at the end of the day that was, pardon the pun, just ducky, things began to fall apart. As I went to the back door to call the children in for the night, I ran into Luke.

"Mom," he said, "something awful's happened." Grimly he motioned me into the garage. In a corner behind a large box was an opening in the cement floor about the size of a tennis ball. From far below, sad peeps arose. Luke shone his flashlight down the hole, but the deep darkness swallowed its light.

"Quacks is down there," Luke said in a sick monotone. "He ran off from the rest and I chased him in here."

A series of heartbreaking peeps came from the depths, perhaps as far as ten feet down.

My mind was blank. "I can't think of any way we can get him out," I said.

"That's what I thought," he whispered sadly. We sat for several minutes, helplessly looking down into the small black hold. It seemed clear Quacks would never emerge.

"Come on, Luke," I finally said gently. "These things happen sometimes when you're raising animals."

He turned his flashlight off and walked to the door. "I know," he said. "But he was my favorite."

There was a cloud over us all. As I went to bed I made a mental note to use the sad experience to deepen our kids' understanding of the parable of the lost sheep. Even though there were still eleven ducks, we mourned the loss of that one, just as Jesus mourns the loss of even a single soul.

The garage is right under my bedroom. As the sun rose the next morning I heard those desperate peeps begin again. *Please, God, help me think of a way Quacks can join his brothers and sisters.* I took a breath and lay quietly, envisioning Quacks reunited with his down siblings, waddling off to catch grasshoppers in the garden. . . .

Grasshoppers! If we tied a grasshopper to the end of some fishing line could we entice Quacks to bite and then pull him up? The idea seemed far-fetched, but Luke agreed it was worth a try. As I started breakfast Luke went into the garage. After about twenty minutes he returned.

"Mom, Quacks is biting the grasshopper, but every time I try to lift him he falls back down." There was urgency in his voice. "Please pray," he asked. *"Now."*

As he raced off I put down my spatula. "God," I said, "I know you must love all

Your creatures. We also love them and try to care for them. You made Quacks with feelings, and he is hungry and lonely and scared. If it is Your will, Lord, help us to save him."

Several minutes later Luke came into the house beaming. Snuggled against his chest was a light-brown duck with a soft yellow bib. Quacks! "I pulled him all the way up," Luke said, bubbling with happiness. "When he came to the top he let go of the grasshopper and I grabbed him just before he fell back down."

Over pancakes Luke explained the details to the rest of the family. Tyler wasn't a bit surprised. "In bed last night I prayed for Quacks," he said matter-of-factly. "I know God can do anything."

Including saving wayward creatures that have fallen through the—um—quacks.

"PRAY, MAMA, PRAY!"

KELSEY TYLER

The children's choir had just finished performing that Sunday in December 1983, and Laura Sowers was looking forward to an afternoon with her youngest child Marc. Laura's husband Craig had a business meeting that would take up much of the afternoon and the couple's oldest child, Cara, seven, was going to stay at church for two hours to practice for the upcoming Christmas musical.

"You and I will go have lunch by ourselves," she said, grinning at four-year-old Marc and straightening his blond hair. "It'll be our special afternoon out."

"Oh boy, Mama," Marc said and whirled around, his toy teddy bear Fluffy clutched tightly in one hand. "Can I have French fries?"

Laura laughed. "Of course, silly. Now, come on." She took his hand in hers and headed for the car.

Laura checked her watch as they pulled out of the church parking lot. She needed to be back at two o'clock to pick up Cara. She figured she had enough time to drive to the Broadway Southwest shopping mall in Albuquerque, New Mexico, where she and Marc could have lunch and wander through the Christmas displays.

As Laura drove, she and Marc talked about Sunday school and Christmas trees and a dozen other things that the child enjoyed. As they spoke, Laura was struck by the sincerity of the small boy's faith. He trusted God implicity, and oftentimes when the family found itself in trouble, Marc was the first one to suggest prayer.

Laura smiled. No wonder the Bible said the kingdom of heaven belonged to the little children. They have not had time to become cynical about life, Laura thought. She glanced at Marc, who had grown quiet and was staring out the front window. It was a bright, sunny day but the temperatures were only in the mid-forties. Marc still wore his nylon jacket and the car heater hummed comfortably as they neared the mall.

"I love you, Marc," Laura said.

Marc grinned. "Love you, too, Mama."

Minutes later they arrived at the mall and made their way to the coffee shop on Broadway's third floor. Just outside the doors of the shop was the store's Christmas center, which had been newly decorated with reds, greens and silvers. Live Christmas trees hung with hundreds of lights added to the festive atmosphere.

"Table for two," Laura said, holding Marc's hand and noticing how the boy stood a little taller. He still clutched Fluffy. Marc slept with the well-worn teddy bear and took him everywhere.

"Kinda like a date, huh, Mama," he commented, hugging Fluffy tightly to his chest.

"That's right. Just you and me."

"And Fluffy," Marc added quickly.

"Yes, and Fluffy. We can't forget him."

The waitress led them to a table and they enjoyed a lunch of grilled cheese sandwiches, French fries, and root beer. They giggled about a silly book they'd read the week before and talked in hushed tones about the presents Marc was going to buy his daddy.

Midway through their meal, an older woman approached their table and smiled. Laura noticed there were tears in her eyes.

"I just wanted you to know I've been watching the two of you," she said, her eyes meeting Laura's. "And you have the sweetest relationship with your son." She paused a moment. "Hold on to that, dear. He'll only be little for such a very short time."

Laura's eyes grew dim as she thought back to the days when Marc and Cara were babies. The woman wasn't telling her anything she didn't already know. Indeed, the time when her children would be young was passing quickly and Laura was intent on making the most of it.

"Thank you," she said. "You certainly are right. They grow up all too quickly."

The woman nodded and looked once more at Marc. Then she bid them goodbye and headed out of the restaurant on her way through the mall.

Fifteen minutes later, when they had shared an ice cream sundae, scraping the bowl clean, Laura and Marc stood to leave. He tucked his small sticky hand in hers and grabbed his teddy bear with the other. Then they walked in the direction of the Christmas shop.

"Oh, Mama, it's so pretty," Marc said, his eyes wide with excitement as he looked from one tree to another.

They walked through the shop, stopping to watch a toy train circle around the base of one of the trees, and again to watch an animated Santa Claus. Finally, it was 1:20 and reluctantly the twosome headed for the escalator that would take them down two stories to the main level, where they had parked.

Marc stepped on the escalator first and Laura followed, taking the step above him so that he was riding down in front of her. Christmas music filled the air and Laura noticed how brightly decorated the store was. It made her wish for Christmas and look forward to the days of preparation which lay ahead.

Suddenly Marc screamed, breaking the peaceful moment and causing a wave of panic to rush through Laura's body.

"Mommy, help!" His voice was filled with fear and he began releasing short screams, crying for his mother to help him.

Laura had no idea what was happening but on Marc's third scream his small body suddenly jerked toward the right so that he was now facing his mother. His eyes were wide with terror.

"Mommy, help me!" he screamed again, this time louder and longer. Suddenly, Laura saw what had happened.

Marc had been wearing deck shoes with thick rubber soles that came up an inch along the sides. As the escalator headed down, Marc had allowed the toe of his foot to be pulled along the non-moving right wall of the escalator. In a matter of seconds the steel surface had grabbed Marc's shoe, sucking it down into the narrow space between the moving escalator stairs and the wall. In doing so it had turned his foot around completely so that the inside of his right foot was now against the escalator wall, buried somewhere beneath the moving stairs.

Laura bent over and saw that her son's foot had disappeared into a space that was not quite half an inch wide. All she could see was the boy's heel. Worst of all the escalator was still moving.

Instantly Laura knew that if they reached the bottom and Marc's foot was still stuck it would be torn into shreds.

She tugged fiercely on her son, hoping to dislodge the foot. But it was being sucked further into the mechanics of the escalator and again Marc screamed in pain. They were only ten steps from the bottom.

For an instant Laura froze, unsure in her panic of what to do next. She needed to stop the escalator but in that moment the task felt impossible, like trying to stop a runaway truck or a tornado.

"Please," Laura shrieked. "Someone stop the escalator!"

There was a flurry of activity at the base of the moving stairs and then, in a matter of seconds, the escalator came to a sudden stop. Most escalators have shut-off buttons located at their base and several people in the vicinity apparently knew this.

Laura released a heavy sigh. "Thank God," she whispered. They were five seconds from reaching the bottom.

Now that the machine was no longer moving, Laura lowered herself onto her knees and examined Marc's foot closely. It had been sucked so far down into the machine that everything but the very edge of Marc's heel was tangled up with the gears and mechanical parts beneath the surface.

Images of Marc going through life with only one foot flashed through Laura's mind. "Dear God," she yelled, "help us! Someone please call the fire department. Please! Call nine-one-one."

Laura looked at the place where Marc's foot should have been and knew with sinking certainty that flesh and bones could not survive this type of accident. Laura's mind was racing. Surely Marc would lose his foot. And what if he was bleeding from the area where his foot might already by missing? He could be bleeding to death and there would be nothing anyone could do for him until the firemen arrived and freed him from the machine.

"Please!" Laura screamed again. "Someone call the fire department!"

Marc was whimpering now, his face ashen. "Mama," he said. He was calmer than before but there was still fear in his voice.

"Pray, Mama, pray!"

Suddenly Laura realized that Marc was right. "That's exactly what we need to do, honey," she said. "Pray with me."

In the past, Laura had always been nervous about praying aloud. She did not seek out attention and did her best to avoid being at the center of visible events. Now, though, with Marc's foot trapped in the escalator, Laura could think of nothing but helping her son. Even though she couldn't concentrate on exactly what to say, she prayed aloud, asking God to help them. Then she began quoting from Romans 8:28 in the Bible. "All things work for good to those who love the Lord," she said loudly. "You promised, Lord, you promised. Please work everything out here, please!"

Marc squirmed painfully and large teardrops rolled down his face. "Mommy, my bones are all broken and bleedy," he said.

In that moment, Laura wondered if she would survive the ordeal. Her vision was growing dim and she felt light-headed. I *can't faint*, she told herself. Not *now*.

"Please, God, don't let me pass out," she said aloud. "Marc needs me too much."

Her hearing began to fade and she shook her head, furiously trying to maintain consciousness. "God, please help me!" she said, her voice loud and steady. "I know You're here, Jesus, but where are You? I need real help right now!"

Laura had her arms around Marc, holding him up since his foot was trapped at such a strange angle. At that instant, soothing arms wrapped themselves around Laura's back. She glanced down and saw the shoes of an older woman dressed in polyester pants.

"Jesus is here," she cooed, speaking softly into Laura's ear. "Jesus is here. He's going to help you."

Instantly the faint feeling disappeared and Laura sat a bit straighter, still holding Marc as tears filled her eyes.

"Tell your son his foot is fine," she said. Her voice was utterly peaceful and Laura felt her body begin to relax.

"Go ahead," the woman repeated. "Tell your son his foot is fine."

Laura wondered at the wisdom of saying those words to Marc. After all, his foot was twisted into a tiny space, caught by the grinding teeth of an escalator. What reason did she have to believe that her son's foot would be fine? Laura began to voice her doubts but the woman sounded so reassuring and somehow familiar that she simply did as she was told.

"Marc, honey," she began. "Jesus is here with us. Mama prayed and He's right here. Your foot is going to be fine, honey."

Laura saw that the boy looked overheated in the jacket and she began to remove it from his shoulders.

"No," the woman said, speaking almost directly into Laura's ear. "Leave the jacket on."

Again Laura did as she was told.

"Mama, my foot hurts," Marc began crying harder. "My bones are all broken and bleedy, Mama."

"Tell him there are no broken bones," the woman whispered, her voice calm and reassuring.

Laura didn't hesitate this time. "Marc, your foot isn't broken, honey. It's going to be just fine."

"I want my daddy!" Marc cried. "Daddy! Daddy come get me!"

Laura lifted her head and shouted Craig's business number. "Someone, please call my husband and ask him to come at once!"

Again there was a commotion as people responded to the urgency of the situation. Laura ran her hand along Marc's hair. "It's all right, honey. Daddy's coming."

Marc sniffled loudly and turned to face Laura, his blue eyes wide with pain. "I'm so glad this isn't happening to you, Mommy." He wiped at his tears with his free hand, holding Fluffy tightly in the other. "I'm sorry about my shoes."

Once more the woman whispered into Laura's ear. "Tell him you'll get him new shoes," she said.

For a moment Laura pictured shopping for shoes with a son who had only one foot. She banished the thought from her mind. "Honey, you can have new shoes when your foot's all better. Whatever kind you want."

Marc turned toward his mother once more and there was a hint of a smile. "Could I get cowboy boots like Daddy's?"

Laura nodded, praying that he would have both feet to wear them on. "Just like Daddy's," she said.

At that instant, the fire department arrived and in a flurry of motion they used crowbars to pull back the escalator wall and free Marc's foot.

Laura held her breath as the fireman removed the shredded remains of Marc's deck shoe and then the tattered sock. His foot was bruised but it wasn't bleeding. The skin had not even been broken.

"I can't believe it," the fireman uttered. He looked at Laura. "I don't want to tell you how bad I thought this was going to be."

The man's partner stepped closer and examined the foot. "I'd say that's nothing short of a miracle," he said. "You need to get him to the hospital for X-rays. But I think he's going to be fine."

Laura looked up to find the woman who had comforted her during the ordeal. But all she saw was the woman's shoes and the lower part of her polyester pant legs as she rounded the corner and disappeared.

Strange, Laura thought. *She didn't even stay to see if she was right about Marc's foot being okay.*

Craig met them at the base of the escalator then and they drove to the hospital while Laura explained what had happened.

"We were having such a wonderful day," she cried, tears of relief filling her eyes. "And then this happened."

Craig reached across the car and took Laura's hand. "There's nothing you could have done, honey. Don't blame yourself."

"I know. It's just that you think your child should be perfectly safe in that situation and then all of a sudden we were in the middle of an emergency."

She paused a moment. "You know, I was too frantic to pray until Marc asked me to. He was the one who knew we had to pray."

Then Laura told Craig about the mysterious woman who had comforted her and told her that Marc's foot would be fine.

"She said there were no broken bones," Laura pondered. "Then she left just before they pulled his foot out."

"Well, I'm sure she was a sweet lady but we'll have to see about the broken bones. His foot is pretty swollen."

Thirty minutes later they were sitting in the emergency room of the hospital. The doctor listened carefully to Laura's description of what happened to Marc.

"His foot isn't broken," Laura told the doctor. "I just know it isn't."

The doctor raised an eyebrow doubtfully. "We'll let the X-rays be the judge of that."

In less than an hour they had the results of the X-rays and the doctor grinned in disbelief. "I can't believe a person could have his foot sucked into a moving escalator and not break any bones, but you were right. The X-rays are perfectly normal."

Laura pulled Marc into a hug and glanced up at her husband. "Whoever that lady was, she was right about everything she said, especially the most important thing."

"What was that?"

"She said Jesus was with us. Marc and I prayed for that and I know for sure He was there," she said. "Right when we needed Him."

ANSWERED PRAYER

JODIE BERNDT

Gary Gilliam knew he served a miracle-working God, and he had heard plenty of stories that revealed the connection between miracles and prayer. Yet he had never seen or been a part of a miracle himself. He wanted to, though, so he decided to ask God to show him a miracle.

Gary prayed, and he expected God to hear him. Even so, he was startled one morning when, at five o'clock, a powerful, loving voice interrupted his slumber. "My son," the voice said, "I want you to go to a small town in Georgia, just south of Jackson, and look for that Pentecostal Lutheran."

Rubbing the sleep from his eyes, Gary struggled to comprehend the message. He and his wife ran a nondenominational church camp, and they had met people from all religious backgrounds. Never had he encountered anyone who called himself a "Pentecostal Lutheran." Gary couldn't help but be a bit skeptical.

"God," he said, "if that's really You, tell me something else."

By now Gary was wide awake, and there was no mistaking the audible voice that filled his room. "You'll go to Georgia, you'll drive a green car and you'll talk to ten men."

Instead of clearing things up, that answer only added to Gary's confusion. He didn't even own a car—much less a green one. And besides, Jackson was more than six hundred miles away. Nonetheless, Gary knew he had heard the voice of God, and he sensed that his miracle was about to happen.

A few days later the first piece of the puzzle fell into place when Gary's brother-in-law got a new car and offered Gary his old one. It was a green Chevrolet. With no real idea as to where he was headed, Gary packed his bags, kissed his wife good-bye and headed south to Georgia.

He drove all night. The next morning, as he pulled into Jackson, Gary realized the senselessness of his position. He wanted to see a miracle, but he had no idea where to turn. He continued to pray, and driving slowly through the town, he pulled into a church parking lot, where he met one of the pastors. Gary asked him if he knew any Pentecostal Lutherans.

The man looked quizzically at Gary before answering. "I've never heard of a Pentecostal Lutheran. But if you'll come into my office, I'll make a few phone calls."

Gary followed the pastor into the church, where a number of calls failed to turn up any leads. No one, it seemed, knew anyone who could be considered a Pentecostal Lutheran. Finally, however, another pastor offered a clue. "We don't have any Pentecostals in this town," he said, "at least none that I know of. But a few years ago a couple who visited our church started some sort of home fellowship group on the outskirts of town. They might know something."

Grateful for any lead, no matter how slim, Gary drove to the couple's house. A woman answered his knock, and he introduced himself. "My name is Gary. I just drove up in a green car. Does that mean anything to you?"

The woman immediately locked her screen door, but as Gary explained his situation, she seemed to soften. "You'll want to talk to my husband," she said. "He's meeting with several men down at Bob Long's Chevrolet dealership."

Gary was beginning to feel his lack of sleep when he reached the car lot and introduced himself to a small group of men. "I'm looking for a Pentecostal Lutheran," he said. Gary had repeated the phrase so often that it rolled easily off his tongue. Even so, the men could not think of anyone who fit the unusual description.

Sensing Gary's fatigue, one of the men invited him to join his family for dinner and then spend the night in an apartment behind his house. Later that evening, during dinner, the telephone rang. It was Bob Long, the fellow who owned the car dealership. He sounded excited.

"My wife and I just realized something," he said. "My grandfather was a Lutheran minister. I was raised Lutheran—but now I'm Pentecostal. *I'm the guy!*"

Bob invited Gary to come to his house and meet his wife Mary. Gary accepted and, thanking his hosts for the meal, he grabbed his jacket and his Bible. He arrived at the Longs' home, still uncertain as to why he was there. He met Mary and the Longs' two young sons. Then, not knowing what else to say, he invited the couple to pray.

Gary began a general sort of prayer, and then, before he could stop himself, he heard himself describing a litany of arguments and destructive patterns that marked the couple's marriage. Gary knew he ought to be embarrassed to speak of the intimate details in these strangers' relationship, but he felt compelled to continue.

Bob and Mary sat dumbfounded by what they heard. There was no denying that their unusual guest spoke the truth—*but how could he know such things?* Old wounds and communication problems paled beside Gary's powerful words, and Bob and Mary did not need to exchange looks to know what each was thinking: God had sent a total stranger six hundred miles to get their attention, and His message was right on the mark.

Gary continued speaking until sometime after midnight. As they soaked up his words, the change in Bob and Mary was unmistakable. Gary could tell something incredible was taking place. Bob and Mary's marriage was being healed.

The following day Gary began his drive home. It was raining, but nothing could dampen his enthusiasm. He had heard God's voice, which was miracle enough, he thought. He had gone to Georgia, driven a green car and talked with . . . yes, he realized, *exactly ten men*. Even more wonderful, though, was that he had been privileged to serve as God's messenger. He had seen the Lord restore a marriage right before his eyes.

Gary slowed down to navigate his car through the rain. As he did, he heard God speak again. "I sent you there to answer that little boy's prayers."

He became confused. What, he wondered, did that mean? Unable to answer his own question, Gary tucked God's words away in the back of his mind. One more missing puzzle piece.

This time, Gary did not have to wait for an answer. A letter arrived from the Longs, describing how their seven-year-old son Aaron had stood up in church. "Mom and Dad used to fight all the time," the child had said, "and I used to get out of bed and pray. I knew my Jesus could help."

Gary read the words over again. *I knew my Jesus could help.* Little Aaron had prayed for his parents, just as Gary had asked God to show him a miracle. Gary smiled to himself. *How very like God to use one miracle to answer two different prayers.*

LOST AND FOUND

ANN SPANGLER

Alan Smith and his wife Leisa had spent part of the day raking leaves and pine straw from his mother-in-law's backyard. His young daughter Lydia was helping grandma too, in typical four-year-old fashion. They worked hard through the afternoon and as twilight edged across the horizon, they straightened their backs, stretched and looked with satisfaction on their handiwork.

The yard looked great. The huge pine trees shimmered green against the deepening blue sky. Beautiful as they were, these trees had made a mess of the yard, yielding twelve bags full of pine straw. Now the black lawn bags were piled together in the middle of the grass.

Their sense of satisfaction was cut short as Leisa suddenly exclaimed, Oh, no! My ring is gone. It could be anywhere on the lawn or in one of these bags." Her diamond engagement ring had slipped off her finger as she worked.

"We all felt sick, but I decided we could do something about it," explained Alan. "So I said, 'Let's just pray right now. God knows where it is.' We sat down on the grass and asked him to show one of us where the ring was. We closed our eyes and just stayed quiet for a minute. Suddenly, my four-year-old jumped up and said, 'I know where it is!' She walked over to all those bags of pine straw and pulled one out.

It wasn't the first one or the one on the edge either. Lydia went to one in the middle of all the bags and said, 'Open this one.' We didn't even have to dump the contents out. As soon as I opened it and spilled a little of the straw, out came the ring!"

What a wonderful experience for this small family! To pray together for their need and to see God use the tiniest member to perform a miracle. That day, the Smith family rejoiced, not just because something of value was restored to them but because something very precious was added to their faith.

Chapter 2   God Keeps Me Safe

It was a time of great danger in Egypt. The Pharaoh had become afraid of the great numbers of Hebrews in Egypt, and when his systematic, oppressive use of slave labor failed to control their numbers, he ordered that their infant boys be killed at birth. The Hebrew midwives and mothers were naturally uncooperative, resorting to creative deceptions and strategies to save their sons. One mother devised a clever plan to save her son. She took a papyrus basket and covered it with tar and pitch to make it waterproof. She tucked her infant son into the basket, then placed it in the reeds of the Nile where she knew it would be discovered by the Pharaoh's daughter. This intrepid mother left her own daughter to watch the baby. When the child was discovered, the Pharaoh's daughter had him pulled out of the water and the sister Miriam stepped forward, volunteering to find a wet nurse for the child. The infant was therefore reunited with his mother, to be raised until he was old enough to be returned to the court of Pharoah.

Of course, this is the story of how the infant Moses was kept safe from the threat of death. Ironic, isn't it, that the destructive plans of the evil Pharaoh were doomed by a conspiracy of women. For these mothers and daughters, keeping an infant safe was instinctive. And weren't they creative? God's fingerprints are all over these events as each woman did her part to protect this child.

Undoubtedly Moses heard the story of his dramatic rescue many times while growing up, and knew that his very life was dependent on God's safe-keeping. When the time came, Moses played his own significant role in God's plan to save the Hebrews from their oppressive bondage in Egypt. God had promised the Hebrews safe passage to their own home, their own land. Moses, who was once kept safe as an infant, now delivered his people to the safety God had promised. The man remembered what the child knew, that God keeps us safe.

> Fear of man will prove to be a snare,
> but whoever trusts in the LORD is kept safe.
>
> —Proverbs 29:25

ALWAYS NEAR

JOAN WESTER ANDERSON

Eileen Bosshart of Streamwood, Illinois, was in the middle of a dilemma. She had run out of a major ingredient for tonight's dinner, and if she ran to the store for it, the meal would be late—and she'd be even later for tonight's choir practice. Oh, there were times when it was difficult being the mother of nine! Eileen's days were spent chauffeuring children in all directions, while trying to keep up with housework and her own projects—editing a newsletter, teaching religion classes, helping run a food pantry in an inner-city parish and, at this particular time, planning a dinner dance to raise funds for a missionary priest. "I tried to fit in as many activities as I could in a day," Eileen says, in modest understatement. "But I always seemed to be rushing."

Now she searched through kitchen cabinets, slamming doors and pulling out drawers. Surely she could find something to substitute! The thought of another errand at this busy time of day was too much to contemplate.

But her hopeful searching yielded nothing, so the supermarket dash was inevitable. The youngest, four-year-old Allison, had been watching Eileen's frenetic search and realized that Mom was going out. "Can I come with you, Mommy?" Eagerly the little girl ran to the back door.

Eileen couldn't let herself be slowed down by a preschooler. Time was crucial. If she could get to the store, find what she needed in a hurry and race home, she could resume her fast track without too much of a loss. "Not now, Allison." Eileen brushed past her daughter. "You stay here and watch television with Danny and Mark. I'll take you another time when I'm not in such a hurry."

The station wagon was parked in the driveway. Her thoughts scattered, Eileen rushed out, climbed in and started the engine. Quickly she shifted into reverse. At least, she *tried* to, but the gear seemed to be stuck. She tried again, pulling with all her might, but the lever wouldn't move. Oh no, not now, not when she most needed to save time! Why did everything seem to go wrong when she was in a hurry?

At that moment, Eileen heard a little tapping sound. And as she looked through the rearview mirror, time seemed to stand still. The top of Allison's blond head was barely visible through the back window, but Eileen could see her daughter standing directly behind the station wagon, almost against it. Had the gear not stuck, she would have roared backward down the driveway, right over her child.

"Oh, Allison!" Eileen stumbled out of the car, scooped up her daughter and put her in the front seat. What a near miss! "I sat and held her and prayed for a couple of minutes, until I felt my strength coming back," Eileen says. "Then I put the car in reverse again. The gear moved easily, and we backed safely out of the driveway."

Was it coincidence that the reverse gear stuck once—and never again during many additional years of driving? "I know that God is attentive to us whether we are consciously thinking of Him or not," Eileen says. "I'll be forever grateful that He spared us all from such a tragedy."

THE "GOOD FEAR" ANGEL

CHARLIE W. SHEDD

My name is David and I will tell you a story about what happened to me at my grandmother's house last summer. I do not have a father, so my mother has to work very hard sewing clothes at the factory. In the summer I go to stay with my grandmother. She lives on a farm quite a long ways from us. She has a pony named Alice. Alice is black and white and can run very fast.

My best friend in the summer is Wallace. We met in Sunday School at my grandmother's church. He lives three miles away, so I ride Alice to see him. It is a safe road to ride because hardly anything but small trucks come on our road. This is because the bridge is old and not safe for big trucks. I love to ride fast because I like to hear the sound of Alice's hooves on the pavement and I like it most when we go across the bridge.

One day Wallace and I were playing and I forgot to leave on time. That meant I was going to be late getting home to grandmother's and she would worry. So I was riding faster than ever. All of a sudden Alice stopped and I nearly flew over her head!

She had never done that before! Nothing I did would make her move. I kicked her in the side, I switched her with my reins, I scolded her, which I hardly ever do.

Finally I got off and looked around for something that might have scared her. Then I walked up to the bridge, and what do you think? The bridge had fallen in! It had broken in the middle and, if Alice hadn't stopped, we might have been hurt bad. We might even have been killed is what some people said.

I put some big limbs on my side of the broken bridge to warn everyone else. Then I went back to Wallace's house and called my grandmother. She came to get me by a different road. My grandmother didn't scold me, so on the way home I asked her, "How did Alice know the bridge had fallen in?"

Grandmother said there are special angels she calls "Good Fear" Angels. Sometimes it is a good thing to be afraid because that will keep you from dangers you should be afraid of. Sometimes, she said, being afraid like that is a gift from God. Then she told me another thing. The Good Fear Angel probably knew I wouldn't listen because I was in too big a hurry. So the Good Fear Angel told Alice to stop instead of trying to tell me.

I like that, don't you? I am glad angels really are smarter than I am and sometimes ponies are, too. That is a good thing, isn't it?

THE SNAKEBITE

DEBBIE DURRANCE

We had just finished Sunday dinner when our twelve-year-old son Mark asked if he and his dog Bo could go out into the field beyond our house for a while. "Just be careful," my husband told him. It was the advice Bobby always gave our children whenever they went out alone, especially in the three years since we'd moved thirty miles out into the brushland of southwestern Florida. Several of our animals had been bitten by rattlesnakes.

As I cleared away the dinner dishes, I watched Mark and Bo race off through the orange and lemon trees of our private oasis. Mark had become so self-reliant out here in the country, I thought.

I took my time with the dishes, enjoying the slow Sunday afternoon, and was just finishing up when I heard the living room door open. Suddenly our older son Buddy yelled, "Mark, what's wrong?"

I threw down the dish towel and ran toward the living room just as Mark gasped, "I—I've been rattlesnake bit—" There was a dull thud. When I got there, Mark was on the floor, unconscious.

"Go get your dad. Hurry," I said to Buddy.

I pulled off Mark's shoe; his foot had already swollen into a large, ugly purple mass. There was a musky odor about him, the same odor we'd noticed the times our animals had been bitten by rattlesnakes. In seconds, Bobby rushed in and grabbed Mark up in his arms. "Come on," he said. "We've got to get him to the emergency center."

We ran and climbed into the cab of Bobby's work truck. I held Mark on my lap, Buddy sat in the middle and Bobby drove. "O God," I prayed, "help us." It was seventeen miles to the emergency center, and every minute counted.

Mark was unconscious, and convulsions jerked his body. I tried to hold him still, with his face close to mine. As long as I could feel his breath against my cheek, I knew he was still alive. But the soft flutters were becoming weaker and less frequent.

"Hurry, Bobby—please hurry!" I pleaded as he frantically passed car after car. Buddy sat in the center, quietly struggling to hold his brother's legs. None of us dared say it, but we all knew we were in a race with death.

As we neared the business section, steam started to seep out from under the hood of the truck. The motor was overheating. About a mile from the clinic, the motor began to pop and sputter.

I glanced over at Bobby. What would we do if the motor stopped? But before I could get the words out Bobby had to brake for a slower vehicle and the motor cut off completely. I clutched Mark to me, trying to hold on to whatever life was left.

We were right in the middle of traffic. Cars were pulling around us and honking their horns. Bobby jumped out and tried to flag down one of the motorists, but the cars just sped around him. "Why won't they stop?" Buddy sighed.

Desperate by now, Bobby ran over and pulled Mark from my arms. He carried him out to the rear of the car, where the other drivers could see him, but still the cars kept going by. Finally one old compact car stopped. The driver appeared to be a Haitian farm worker, and he didn't understand English. But he could tell we needed help.

"Thank you, thank you . . . " Bobby shouted as he pulled open the door and pushed Buddy in the backseat. Then he laid Mark down beside him and waved the driver off as I jumped in the front.

"We have to get to the emergency center," I cried, but the driver's questioning look told me he didn't understand. I pointed in the direction we should go.

As we pulled away, I glanced back at Bobby standing in the street. There was no room for him in the small car and our truck was blocking traffic, but I wished he could be with me.

At the emergency center, medical technicians started working on Mark immediately, trying to stabilize his condition. They started fluids and began artificial respiration. But soon after Bobby arrived, the emergency technicians told us they had done all they could and were transferring Mark to Naples Community Hospital, where Dr. Michael Nycum would meet us.

By the time we arrived at the hospital, Mark had stopped breathing twice and had gone into a coma. For the next twelve hours we waited and prayed while the doctors and nurses worked constantly with him. We could tell by the looks on their faces that they didn't expect him to make it.

"Folks, about the only thing the little fellow has going for him is his heart—and that's under tremendous strain," Dr. Nycum told us.

We watched helplessly during the next twenty-four hours as the venom attacked every part of his body. His eyes swelled so tight that all we could see were the ends of his eyelashes. His leg was so swollen the doctors had to make long slashes along it to relieve the pressure on the blood vessels. And still they were afraid they might have to amputate.

Then, miraculously, Mark passed the crisis point and began to improve a little. He was still in a coma, and certainly not out of danger, but the swelling began to go down.

After that, each day brought improvement. On Thursday, Bobby and I sat there beside Mark's bed. We were drained, exhausted, prayed out. I was sitting in a chair close to him, holding his hand, when I thought I felt a movement. But no, I told myself, it was probably my imagination. Yet a moment later, there it was again, a faint fluttering of the small hand inside mine.

"Bobby," I said, sitting up and reaching across to him, "Bobby! Mark moved—he moved!"

Bobby summoned the nurses and doctor. Mark was coming out of the coma.

"Mom . . . Mom . . ." he moaned.

"Yes, honey, we're here." The words caught in my throat.

"Dad . . ."

"Yes, son . . ."

His eyes opened now as he looked over at Bobby. "Dad . . . are you mad at me?"

"What do you mean?" Bobby tried to laugh, but it came out a little ragged. "Of course I'm not mad at you."

"I was afraid you'd be mad at me for being so careless."

Bobby reached over and patted Mark on the head. "We're just thankful you're getting better. But what happened, Son? Do you feel like telling us?"

The nurses and Dr. Nycum moved a little closer.

"Well, Bo and I spotted a bird in a cabbage palm and, well, I guess I wasn't paying too much attention to where I was going. I was looking at the bird and jumped over the ditch . . . and my foot landed on something that moved when I hit it.

"And then it was like something slammed down hard on my foot, and my leg started getting real hot. When I looked down, I saw a big rattler had hold of my shoe—it was biting on my foot. It was hurting so bad and Bo was barking and jumping at the snake, but it wouldn't let go. Then Bo jumped on the snake and tore into its head. It let go and crawled off into the bushes.

"Dad, I tried to remember what you said to do if we ever got snakebit, but I was hurting so bad, and getting weak and dizzy. I was a long way from the house, and I knew none of you would hear if I called . . ."

"But where were you, Mark?" Bobby asked.

"Out in the field, a long ways from the house. Out there next to the ditch in the field."

"But that's a third of a mile from the house. How did you get to the house?"

Dr. Nycum shook his head. "Medically speaking it would have been impossible for him to walk that far."

Bobby and I looked uncertainly at each other. There were also the thirteen steps up to our front door—he'd had to climb those too. I took a deep breath. After everything that had happened, I was almost afraid to ask, but I had to know, "How did you get back to the house, Mark?"

"Well, I remembered you and Dad saying that the more you moved, the quicker the poison would reach your heart, and I knew I couldn't run. But I was so scared, and all I wanted to do was *get* home. I probably would have run if I could have, but I couldn't because it hurt so bad. And then . . . Dad, there's something I have to tell you. About the man."

"The man? What man?" Bobby asked. "Was someone out there with you?"

"Yes—I mean, no—I mean, I don't know. All I know is that he carried me . . .'"

"He carried you?"

"Yes, when I couldn't make it to the house. He picked me up." I could feel a tingle on the back of my neck.

"He talked to me in a real deep voice," Mark went on, "and told me that I was going to be real sick, but that I'd be all right."

"What did he look like?" I asked Mark shakily.

"I couldn't see his face, Mom. All I could see was that he had on a white robe, and his arms were real strong. He reached down and picked me up. And I was hurting so bad, I just sort of leaned my head over on him. He carried me to the house and up the steps. When he put me down, I held on to the door and turned around, and—"

His blue eyes stared into mine with an earnestness I'd never seen before. "All I could see was his back."

For a long time, none of us could speak; it was almost more than we could take in. "God is our refuge and strength," I said to myself, "an ever present help in trouble" (Psalm 46:1).

For most of my life I had believed that passage in the Bible by faith. Now I saw the proof of it.

"Mom ... Dad ..." Mark said, hesitating. "I know you may not believe me—"

"We believe you," I whispered as Bobby put his arm around me. "We believe you."

THE LAST CHRISTMAS GIFT

JOAN WESTER ANDERSON

Snow had not been predicted. But twelve-year-old Betty Wohlfert (now Roberts) and her ten-year-old sister Leonie didn't give it a thought on that late afternoon in 1924, when they sneaked out with the sled they had just received for Christmas. "Dad thought we were in the house helping Mama, and she thought we were in the barn doing chores for Dad," Betty says. Instead the girls went to a hill near their farm in Hubbardston, Michigan.

Exhilarated and breathless, neither noticed snowflakes starting to fall—until the moon disappeared and gale-force winds began to blow across the darkening landscape. Abruptly, they found themselves in the midst of a blinding blizzard.

Leonie began to cry, tears freezing on her cheeks. She tried to talk, but the angry wind tossed her words away. "Don't cry, Leonie," Betty clung to her sister, attempting to comfort her, but she was frightened too. She had lost all sense of direction and had no idea where the house was. Were they going to freeze here?

"Hey!" a male voice unexpectedly pierced the silence. "You two need help! Hop on the sled and hang on tight—I'll get you home!"

Who was it? Whirling snow made it impossible to see. "But you don't know where our house is," Betty called. Hadn't their father warned them about going with strangers?

"Sure I do!" he shouted back.

Why, it was Joe, Joe Martin! Joyfully, Betty recognized the voice of the seventeen-year-old who lived a mile down their road, one of the kindest people they knew. How lucky to have met him on this out-of-the-way hill!

"Get on the sled," Joe told them again, and both girls obeyed. They could just make out his tall silhouette as he bent to pick up the rope. Then they were off, clinging to each other as Joe pulled them across the fields.

Without his guidance, they surely would have missed the light from their kitchen window—even familiar markers were blurred and confusing in the whirling snow. But Joe stopped right at the back door. "You're home," he called over the gusts, hardly out of breath. "Jump off and get inside."

"Come in and get warm, Joe," Betty called as she waded through the drifts.

But no one answered. Joe was already gone.

A few days later, the girls went with their father to the Martin house. Mrs. Martin welcomed them, led them down the hall, then opened a door. Everyone looked inside.

"Joe, I came to thank you for taking such good care of my daughters," Betty's father told him.

Joe and his mother looked confused.

"The night before last, Joe," Betty prompted, "when you found us and brought us home."

"Nobody in his right mind would have gone out in that storm," Mrs. Martin protested, "especially Joe."

"But—"

"You see, he's been very ill with the flu," she went on, as Joe nodded weakly. "I've been at his bedside almost every moment. He hasn't been out of this room, much less outside, for the past week."

Betty and Leonie never discovered how Joe Martin managed to be in two places at once. But it was a gift they gladly accepted. Christmas was over—but God had saved the best for last.

A POPE'S BLESSING

MARY FOLEY NIELSEN

A household accident is every mother's greatest fear. Small children move so quickly, faster than our watchful eyes can anticipate. On the fateful day that my baby moved faster than I did, I was thankful that God—and one of His most holy saints—were there to protect little Eileen.

It was almost Christmas in 1973 and I was working at a seasonal job selling toys for a toy company. It required my being out of the house only a few hours a week, and during the time I was away, my husband could supervise the kids' homework and bedtime routines. With seven young children, we were grateful for the extra money, which helped pay household (and Santa's) expenses.

The owner of the toy company had visited Rome earlier that year and had brought back religious medals for all of her employees. Each medal held a relic of Pope John XXIII. Being Catholic myself, I admired Pope John for his gentle nature and lively sense of humor. I promptly mailed a brief thank-you note to my employer and life continued at its busy preholiday pace. My baby Eileen was two years old at the time and was a typical toddler—inquisitive, active, climbing everywhere and getting into everything. I was standing just a few feet away from her in my kitchen when the events unfolded that still cause me to marvel all these years later.

My new medal of Pope John had been sitting on the kitchen counter for a day or two, and I decided to slip it onto my key ring. The door key was on one end of the key ring, and since there was an empty ring on the other end, I attached the medal there, and then left the whole thing on the counter. No sooner had I done so than little Eileen climbed onto the kitchen stool and with amazing speed grabbed it off the counter. Harmless enough—a child playing with a set of keys—but to be on the safe side, I reached out to take them from her. Before I could stop her, she turned and inserted the key into an electric outlet on the control panel of my electric range.

I watched in horror as she jolted through the air and was thrown to the floor. The power in the house went out amid flying sparks. Frantic, I scooped my baby into my arms. Praying as I held her to me, I looked down and saw that her tiny hand was completely black. An electrical burn? I was horrified. But no, her hand was covered with soot that brushed right off.

I was astounded when I realized that Eileen actually seemed to be unharmed. Comforting her as she sobbed and thanking God at the same time, I picked up the key ring, which lay on the metal top of the stove. The key itself was very hot to the touch. To my amazement, the image of Pope John's face was scarred where the medal had touched metal and melted. I was mystified. With such a powerful jolt of electricity, how was it possible that Eileen was unharmed? Suddenly I understood:

because the pope's medal dangled from the opposite end of the key ring, it had touched the top of the stove and grounded it, completing the current of electricity. If only the key had been on the ring, as it had been just moments before the incident, the charge would have been enough to do serious and permanent damage to my baby. My heart told me that angels and saints can intervene with nature in miraculous ways.

Many years have passed, and Eileen is now a college graduate. The medal with the scarred likeness of Pope John XXIII is with me always and means even more to me now than it did years ago. Each time I look at the medal I think about God and His chosen helpers—those who inspire us, guide us and protect us, and sometimes even bear our burdens and take on the scars of our human frailties. The medal is a constant reminder that not all miracles are grand, public events that make the news. As I show people the scars on the face of Pope John, I explain that miracles and blessings come in all sizes and can happen to anyone, anywhere . . . even in a humble kitchen.

DISAPPEARING ROOF

JOHN FITCH

In the summer of 1976, my wife and I moved into a new second-floor apartment. One night my wife was at work and I was watching our two-year-old son. Regrettably, I was watching more TV than paying attention to my son. Suddenly I noticed how quiet it had become. I called out to him—and got no answer. I got up and searched the five-room apartment. My son was nowhere to be seen.

At this point, I was getting frantic. As I passed the front window, my peripheral vision caught a reflection of something outside the window. It was my son out on the flat front porch roof. In the dark, the ceiling light had reflected off his forehead, catching my attention.

It was dark. There was an old-fashioned streetlight on the road that caused a dull shine and cast eerie shadows, barely illuminating much beyond the road. I went to the open window, looked out at the shadowy figure sitting on the roof about five feet away, and collected myself. I knew not to panic and start yelling, which could startle him and cause him to lose his balance. So, in a calm voice, I said, "Son, come here. I want to see you." He crawled over the window. I grabbed him and breathed a sigh of relief. Once inside, I scolded and hugged him, closed the screen and told him to never go out there again.

The next day, when I got home from work, I was still thinking about the incident and the memory of him on that roof. I walked to the window, thanking God for my good fortune the previous night. I looked out to the spot where he had been to relive the traumatic sight etched in my mind. I looked out and saw . . . *no roof*!

In the daylight, there was no roof at the distance I had seen him the previous night, which I guessed to be about five feet out. Even reducing that to four feet for judgment error, he would have still been in the air. The roof was a slim one, only going out about three feet and then dropping off steeply with shingles at about a forty-five-degree angle. If he had been only three feet out (and I don't think he was that close), he would have been right on the edge or down onto those shingles. But when he crawled over to me, he crawled straight over and not up and then over. All I can figure is that he had some type of guardian angel helping him that night, and I thank God for whoever that was!

STEERING CLEAR

JOAN WESTER ANDERSON

When Beth's mother went to visit a friend, she took Beth, age five, and Beth's two little sisters along. The girls played in the big backyard all afternoon, until it was time to go home.

Their car was parked in front of the house and faced down a long steep street. Mommy strapped Beth and three-year-old Meg into the backseat and put ten-month-old Amy up front in her car seat. Then Mommy got in behind the steering wheel. "Oh!" she exclaimed suddenly. "I forgot my coat. I'll be right back, girls." She slipped out the car door, closed it, and hurried back to the house.

A minute passed. Then another. Beth sighed. Mommy was probably saying good-bye to her friend again. Beth knew she wasn't supposed to get out from under the seat strap, but sometimes grown-ups talked for so long. She and Meg wiggled out and got down on the floor in the back to play with their dolls while they waited.

Another minute passed, and then Beth felt the car move forward. Had her mother gotten back inside? She looked up, but she couldn't see the back of her mom's head or even hear the sound of the engine. Beth stood up. Horrified, she realized that the car was rolling down the hill, all by itself! Amy had somehow gotten out of her car seat, crawled across to the driver's seat and shifted the gears (something must have been wrong with the clutch). Ahead of them, about fifty yards away, the street ended, and a river began! They were headed directly for it!

"My babies!" Beth heard her mother scream behind them. Amy started to cry, too, as the car picked up speed. Beth saw a neighbor, who had been cutting his lawn, run toward them, but the car was going too fast for him to reach it.

"Mommy! Mommy!" Beth cried. What if the car rolled into the lake? None of them knew how to swim. What should she do? What *could* she do?

Then, as she stood clutching the top of the backseat, Beth saw the steering wheel begin to turn very slowly to the right. There was no reason for it to move, the street was quite straight, and by now the car was traveling very fast. Yet, through her tears, Beth watched the wheel turn farther and farther and farther . . . as if someone was steering the vehicle off the steep hill.

Soon the car left the pavement and bumped along a grassy strip, moving slower and slower and slower. Then it plowed into a small tree, and stopped. Beth pushed the back door open, got out, and started running up the hill.

"Oh, Beth!" Breathlessly, Mommy and the neighbor reached her at the same time. Mommy gathered Beth into her arms while the man and Mommy's friend ran to the car and pulled Meg and Amy out.

Mommy was now crying as hard as Beth. "Thank You, God!" was all she could say as she hugged each daughter, amazed that they had not been hurt.

For, despite the bump against the tree, none of the girls had sustained any injuries. In fact, as Beth realized afterward, even though baby Amy was no longer in her car seat, she hadn't even bounced around at all. She had stayed quietly on the driver's seat, as if a cushion were around her, sealing her in.

It was only later that Beth told her parents about the steering wheel and how it moved. "Do you think an angel was driving?" she asked.

Her mommy and daddy didn't know what to say. But what other answer could there be?

WHEN WE FALL, IT'S TO A PLACE OF GRACE

DAVID WATERS

It was the day after Thanksgiving. The Stigler family of Memphis was taking a holiday break at Fall Creek Falls State Park. Susan Stigler was standing on the observation deck overlooking the falls, holding a video camera. She didn't want to miss a moment.

Her husband and two teenage sons were about to jump off a cliff. Susan wasn't worried. They'd done it before. They weren't really jumping. They were rappelling down the side using special ropes and devices.

Her eldest son Jon, age seventeen, went first. She watched him through the viewfinder as he slid smoothly down the rope 220 feet from the top of the cliff to the rocky floor below.

Jared, fifteen, was next. She kept the camera on him and she waited for him to leap. He seemed to be hung up for a second or two. Then he jumped and began to slide down the rope. It seemed to Susan that he was going awfully fast. It looked like he was dropping, not sliding twenty-two stories. She kept waiting for him to slow down. He never did. Jared knew he was dropping too fast. He reached behind him to grab the rope and slow his descent. But he wasn't wearing the right gloves. The rope burned his hand. Instinctively, he let go.

Then he hit the ground. He bounced and flipped over. Susan gasped. Jared wasn't moving. She thought he was gone. She thought she had just filmed his death. "Thank You, Lord, for these past fifteen years with Jared," she said to herself. Then he moved.

The Stiglers weren't the only family at the falls that day. Connie Walker of Murfreesboro was there with her family and her sister's. They had been sitting at the bottom of the falls enjoying the view. But it was cold, and the adults were ready to go back up to the inn. The kids wanted to stay. Some people were getting ready to slide down the side of the cliff next to the falls. They stayed and watched one.

"Just one more," Connie's son said.

"One more," said Connie, who was past ready to go. She still wasn't feeling well, physically or otherwise. The car wreck she'd had months before had shaken the kids but had nearly broken her. She'd hurt her neck and back. She was having trouble with the physical aspects of her job. Her doctors kept telling her she was going to have to quit.

She was discouraged about her situation, and more than a bit peeved at God about it. How could she quit? They needed the paychecks. Besides, she loved her work. God put her in that job to help people. Now she had to stop? Connie kept going over it all in her mind as she watched a distant figure prepare to jump off the cliff several hundred feet away.

The jumper seemed to have trouble getting started. Then he dropped like a stone, hit the ground, bounced and flipped. Connie and her family watched in silence and in horror as the stranger lay motionless on rocks below the falls.

"Mom!" Connie's little boy yelled. "Do something!"

Susan saw Jared move. Then she saw other people moving toward him. Glenn, Jared's dad, was rappelling down a rope from the top of the cliff. A friend who had been holding Jared's rope from the bottom was still holding on, trying to keep Jared from moving. A few other people Susan didn't know were slowly making their way around the falls, over slippery rocks, to the spot where Jared lay.

"Please, Lord," Susan said, helplessly high above the scene, "please send someone who knows what to do."

Connie and her sister knew what to do. They were nurses. When they got to Jared, they expected to find a pile of bones and organs. Instead, they found a boy who somehow was alive and in one piece.

Jared was bleeding from his mouth and nose, but not too badly. He was in much pain, but awake and relatively alert. His feet and ankles were twisted and swelling, but he didn't seem to have any broken bones. Still, there was no telling what sort of internal damage he had. He had fallen twenty-two stories onto rocks. He was lying at the bottom of a remote canyon. And the two nurses at Jared's feet had no medical equipment or supplies. They worked with Jared's father to keep Jared still, warm and awake. They made splints for his ankles with their hands and kept his legs elevated with their arms for more than an hour.

While they held Jared in place, someone else held them in place on the slippery, sloping rocks. Connie kept checking Jared's pupils and pulse. Every time his heart would race or crawl, she would pray. "God, You can't let this happen to this boy," she'd say.

Emergency crews finally arrived and took Jared to the hospital. But surgeons never operated. There was no need. Jared was fine. He had a cracked heel bone, a dislocated ankle and torn tendons and ligaments. That was all. Emergency room doctors worked his bones back into place with their hands. His injured ankle wasn't getting enough blood for a while, but the blood soon returned.

He still uses a brace, but only when he plays sports.

"I feel fine. I feel blessed," said Jared, a junior at Cordova High.

"That boy is a walking miracle," said Connie, who now has a picture of Jared on her refrigerator and a fresh perspective.

Jared has healed. So has Connie.

"What happened that day revived my spirits," she said. "I'm not going to worry about my situation. I know God is in control. I had to quit being a recovery room nurse, but I know there are lots of ways I can help people."

Susan has watched the video of Jared's accident a hundred times.

"People have asked how I can stand to watch it," she said. "But in a strange way I find it very comforting. I know there are unseen hands in the video. I have no doubt God and His angels were intervening that day. I can't see them but I know they are there."

Jared's family will celebrate his seventeenth birthday today. They celebrate Thanksgiving every day.

Chapter 3   God Supplies My Needs

It was a miserable time. The country was in chaos: The leaders had abandoned the Lord and begun to worship Baal, the god of the surrounding gentiles. Among the few faithful people left was a prophet named Elijah, who told of a drought that would consume the land. Despite the drought, the Lord provided food and water for Elijah, ultimately sending him to a widow who would feed him.

But the Lord had not informed the widow of this plan. Elijah found her collecting sticks for a fire, and asked her for a small jar of water. "Oh, and while you're at it, could I get some bread?" The woman's answer was direct: "As surely as the LORD your God lives," she replied, "I don't have any bread—only a handful of flour in a jar and a little oil in a jug. I am gathering a few sticks to take home and make a meal for myself and my son, that we may eat it—and die" (1 Kings 17:12).

Imagine how despondent this poor mother felt and how frightened her son must have been. Of course, Elijah was unfazed. He knew that the Lord had promised to meet his needs and had sent him to this desperate family. Elijah reassured her, and then relayed a generous promise: "Don't be afraid. Go home and do as you have said. But first make a small cake of bread for me from what you have and bring it to me, and then make something for yourself and your son. For this is what the LORD, the

God of Israel, says: 'The jar of flour will not be used up and the jug of oil will not run dry until the day the LORD gives rain on the land'" (1 Kings 17:13–14).

So the woman, in faith, gave Elijah the first cake of bread, and as promised, her flour and oil never ran out. She was able to feed herself, her son and Elijah throughout the time of drought. God made a promise to this gentile woman and to her son, and He kept His word. His own people had abandoned Him, yet the Lord, the God of Israel, had found a woman whose faith superseded her circumstances. This woman and her child learned what Elijah knew: God supplies our needs.

> Great are the works of the LORD;
> they are pondered by all who delight in them.
> Glorious and majestic are his deeds,
> and his righteousness endures forever.
> He has caused his wonders to be remembered;
> the LORD is gracious and compassionate.
> He provides food for those who fear him;
> he remembers his covenant forever.
>
> —Psalm 111:2–5

PSALM 81:10

CANDY CHAND

I am the Lord your God, who brought you up out of Egypt. Open wide your mouth and I will fill it.

Only days before, Marta Marquez had heard the sermon based on Psalm 81:10. The Scripture had touched her heart, inspired her and given her hope. She was sure of one thing: God is willing and able to provide for His children. Marta, a young mother of three, was open to miracles, and that day a miracle was exactly what she needed.

It was 1979, and her youngest son Carlos was only a few months old. Marta had just fed Carlos the last drop of formula. As Marta searched the pantry, it was clear that their supply had completely run dry. With her son's feeding time rapidly approaching, the young mother began to panic.

Marta's family was struggling at the time, trying their best to make ends meet. They had survived, like many others, from paycheck to paycheck. But now that paycheck was a day away, and her innocent baby couldn't wait.

Marta set out to solve the problem in the only way she knew how: she prayed. She asked God to provide for Carlos, to care for him as one of His own. Then she asked

Him for another favor: "God, I need encouragement. Please help me find that Scripture from the sermon I recently heard. I have no idea where in the Bible to look."

In faith, Marta opened the Holy Book, and it fell open to the Psalms. She had read only a few verses when, sure enough, she saw it: "Open wide your mouth and I will fill it." That was her answer! It was a sign, the found Scripture, a promise of provision.

As Marta wrapped Carlos in a soft blue blanket, she gently rocked him to sleep. With each swaying motion, she continued to pray. "Please take care of my baby. Please provide for him just like Your Scripture promises." In faith, Marta waited. Then she began to wonder. How would God provide? Would He send formula from a kind benefactor? How would He fill the mouth of this tiny, hungry baby?"

Hours went by, and Carlos continued to rest, undisturbed, in a peaceful slumber. Concerned by his sudden change in feeding schedule, Marta entered her baby's room. She checked on him and observed an answer to prayer: not her usual hungry infant, but a resting, quiet angel, with a distended, full tummy. When Carlos awoke the next morning, he was smiling, happy, refusing even a bottle of water.

That afternoon, Marta's husband returned from work. He had cashed his paycheck and carried armfuls of baby formula. Then, and only then, did her tiny son appear hungry. Marta fed Carlos with joy as she offered thanks for God's faithfulness.

Today, as she reflects back over the years, Marta remains grateful for a promise in Scripture, for the tender filling of her young child, and because God continues to provide her family with "every blessing they can use."

OUR MYSTERIOUS BENEFACTOR

JAN JAKEMAN

My parents struggled to raise their three children in the midst of the Great Depression. Eventually I came along too, the last of the brood, but that was later, after the hardest times were over, according to Mother.

At one point, desperate for work to support his family, my father took a job at a factory quite far from their home in Fairmount, Indiana. That left Mother to care for the children alone for weeks at a stretch. When the youngest, baby Jeannie, woke up coughing one morning in the winter of 1931, Mother kept her bundled up near the coal stove in the living room. "The warm air will soothe you, little one," she promised.

But Jeannie's condition worsened as the day wore on. Her cough seemed to come from a hollow place deep down inside her chest. By nightfall her fever raged. The other two children played quietly, careful not to run or shout or ask Mother too many questions. Even Bonnie, the family dog, seemed to sense something was terribly wrong. My mother feared it was pneumonia. What would she do? She didn't have the five dollars it would take to see a doctor.

Before going to bed, Mother and the two older children—Vangie, age ten, and Johnny, eight—prayed for the baby. Mother held a warm rag of onion poultice to Jeannie's chest. "Please, God, touch this child and make her better."

"Amen," Vangie said.

"Amen," said Johnny.

Mother tucked them in, pulling the covers up around their worried faces and kissing them on the forehead. "Is Jeannie going to be all right, Mama?" Vangie finally asked.

"God won't let anything bad happen to her," Mother said. "He'll watch over our little Jeannie extra-close tonight."

"If she feels better tomorrow, maybe she'd like to play with my best truck," Johnny offered.

Mother's heart sank. Jeannie wasn't going to get well overnight. Don't alarm the children, Mother reminded herself. She forced a smile. "Well, that would be fine, John. You're a good big brother, you are. Now you two go to sleep."

She turned off the light in their room and went back to the kitchen to settle Bonnie in her box. "You keep watch too, you sweet old dog," Mother told her. Then she closed the door between the kitchen and the living room in order to conserve the heat from the coal stove.

Mother took the fretful baby into bed, trying to comfort her as best she could. "God, please stay near this house tonight," she pleaded. She closed her eyes and fell into a fitful sleep. But Jeannie's guardian angel was wide awake. . . .

Near dawn, Mother woke to Bonnie's furious barking. She was scrambling around as if she were after something. What is that dog up to? Mother wondered. She sat up in bed. A kitchen chair crashed to the floor. Footsteps! Someone was in the house! Mother jumped, and hugged her baby tight to her chest. Then she heard the intruder running from the kitchen and across the back porch.

Mother was too frightened to investigate. Instead she hurried out of bed to jam a high-back chair under the knob of the closed living room door.

Bonnie's persistent barking roused Vangie and Johnny from their beds. "Come in with Mama, children. We'll all be warmer sleeping together," she told them. They piled into her bed, careful not to disturb little Jeannie. Mother put her lips to the baby's forehead, which seemed as hot as the coal stove itself.

When daylight arrived, Mother put a sleeping Jeannie into her crib and ventured into the kitchen, the other two youngsters trailing behind. Bonnie immediately jumped from her box and ran in circles about their feet.

"Calm down, Bonnie," Mother said, feeling a chill. The back door was standing wide open. "Bonnie, sit down this instant, girl. Sit!" Mother hurried to shut the door.

"Don't you see, Mama?" Johnny said. "She's trying to tell us something."

Mother scanned the kitchen. Not a thing was missing or out of place—except the chair she'd heard go crashing to the floor. I guess Bonnie saw who did this, Mother thought as she bent over to right the chair.

That's when she noticed something on the floor underneath the table, a crumpled piece of paper. What's this? She reached for it and smoothed it out. "My goodness!" she cried, falling into the chair she'd just placed upright. "A five-dollar bill!"

After a hurried breakfast, Mother bundled up the children for the walk into town to see the doctor. There they learned that Jeannie was perilously close to pneumonia. With medication and the doctor's care, she was soon well again.

Years later whenever my mother told this story, someone always asked about the footsteps, the overturned chair, Bonnie's barking. Who had come into the house in the wee hours of the morning? Was the money left behind on purpose? Without fail Mother would smile and say, "The Lord works in mysterious ways." It was no mystery to Bonnie, of course. She had seen it all. But since the dog couldn't talk, I figure Jeannie's guardian angel tipped over the chair, just to be sure the "mystery" wasn't overlooked.

AN ANGEL PROVIDED MONEY
FOR THE OVERDUE BILL

BRAD STEIGER AND SHERRY HANSEN STEIGER

Sixty years ago, Michael Doyle was born near Ballinasloe, Ireland. He has never forgotten the time that an angel brought his mother the money to pay an overdue bill.

"From her birth, my baby sister Kathleen suffered from a chronic illness, which the doctors said she would one day outgrow—if we could keep her alive," Michael told us. You see, her bronchial tubes would spasm in such a way that the poor child could inhale but she couldn't exhale unless someone gave her artificial respiration."

Little Kathleen was in and out of hospitals and clinics, and when she was home the doctor had to visit no less than three times a week.

"I think we were lucky just to scrape by," Michael said. "Although Da made a fairly good living for us, the hospital and doctor bills nearly ate us up. Mother couldn't go back to work, because Kathleen needed constant looking after."

It was in the winter of 1943 that his mother received the money from the angel.

"I was about seven and Kathleen was three or so, and Mother had ordered heavy woolen snowsuits for us to keep away the cold winter winds," Michael continued. "Mother thought that she might be able to squeeze out the money to pay for them by the end of the month of November, but now here it was the middle of March and the bill was long overdue. She knew that if she didn't manage to pay the bill very soon, Da's wages might be garnisheed."

The bill was only a few Irish pounds, around twenty dollars. But, Michael reminded us, in those difficult days of strict rationing in the midst of the strife and stress of World War II, it was a lot of money for a working-class Irish family to set aside for something "extra" like new snowsuits for the kids. He kept expecting his father to grouse about how he and Kathleen could have made do for another winter, but the good man held his peace about the matter.

And then their little miracle occurred.

Mrs. Doyle kept a fern on a stand near the front door, and Michael remembered the day that it suddenly began to shed its leaves.

"It's looking disgraceful, it is," she worried aloud to Michael. "Help me move it back away from the front door. When the weather is warmer, I'll plant it in the yard for the summer."

Michael recalled that his mother lifted the plant, and he flexed his seven-year-old muscles to move the stand.

"As I did so, the doily that had been under the plant slipped off the stand and an envelope that had been under the doily fell to the floor," Michael remembered.

"Strangely enough, it was an airmail envelope, and when Mother opened it, she pulled out crisp, new Irish pound notes—enough to pay her bill at the store and maybe just a wee bit extra."

Michael said that his mother was firmly convinced that God had heard her prayers and had sent an angel to deliver the desperately needed money. It was certain that neither of his parents had put the money under the fern for safekeeping and then forgotten about it. Money was far too scarce in the Doyle household to misplace a single cent, to say nothing of squirreling away any of it.

And they didn't know anyone who could have sent them an airmail letter. Besides, the envelope was unaddressed.

Da and Michael agreed with Mother. The money had come from the angels.

"I always thought the airmail envelope was a very nice touch," Michael said. "After all, the money had come to us through the air from on high."

"MIJO, THE LORD WILL PROVIDE"

ISAAC J. CANALES

It was the one day of the year Mama didn't put beans and tortillas or even her specialty—tamales—on the table. When it came to celebrating Thanksgiving we were as American as anybody else. Cranberry sauce, pumpkin and mincemeat pies, turkey, mashed potatoes and gravy—all that and stuffing too. Mama made the best.

But the year I was eleven we hadn't even begun our holiday preparations by the time the end of November rolled around. And I knew why.

Papa and Mama were pastors of a little church in Keystone (now Carson), California. We were poor—so poor our rent in the projects, twenty-six dollars a month, was almost more than we could handle. We lived on whatever the congregation could afford to give. That autumn times were hard for everyone, and offerings hit an all-time low. I watched the tambourine we used for a collection plate very, very closely.

Nervously I asked Mama about our Thanksgiving dinner. "Isaac, God will provide," she replied. "You know He has always been faithful to us." I remembered the shoes, winter coats, even parts for the family car, that had arrived just when we needed them. Maybe Mama was right. But time was running out. I waited anxiously for something to happen.

Soon the holiday was upon us. I could hear the tambourine rattle dully as a few meager coins hit the skin. Why hasn't God stepped in? I wondered.

I asked Mama again if we would have turkey. "Mijo," she said (meaning "my son"), "the Lord will provide. Has He ever let us down?"

That kept me quiet until Tuesday. Papa and I went to McCoy's Market for groceries to get us through the week—a dozen eggs, tortillas, milk. While he was at the checkout I hurried to the meat department to look at the "toms," as Mama called them. Wistfully I ran my hand over the plump, frozen birds. It wouldn't be Thanksgiving without a turkey.

Wednesday night we gathered in our church, a gutted two-bedroom house with a sign in black-and-yellow letters that read Mision Ebenezer Asamblea de Dios. I watched the regulars assemble: Sister Ayala, with her colorful shawl draped around her shoulders; Brother Garcia, who worked in the orchards; and Sister Audrey, a six-foot-two-inch, seventy-two--year-old former B-movie extra who played the violin and wore a dark fur coat. My family and a few others made up the rest of the congregation that evening.

I tugged on Mama's sleeve as she headed up to the little blue pump organ next to the pulpit. "I know there won't be enough for Thanksgiving dinner," I said. "What are we going to do?"

"*Shh*," she whispered, looking serene as always. "Don't worry, mijo, the Lord will provide." If that were true wouldn't he have done something by now?

The service began. Mama played the organ, Papa strummed the guitar and Sister Audrey joined in on her violin as we sang "There Is Power in the Blood" in Spanish. Papa spoke about the holiday being a time to give thanks to the Lord for His provision. Then he called me: "Isaac, would you please pick up the tithes and offerings tonight? And would you ask the Lord to bless them?"

It was an honor to be asked to participate in the service, but it was the last thing I wanted that night. I mumbled a prayer for the few coins I knew were all that would be forthcoming. After I said amen and raised my head, my eyes caught the glitter of a shiny black car pulling up in front of the church. It was the longest and newest car I had ever seen. The door opened and a tall, handsome man dressed in a tuxedo stepped out. He looked like Clark Gable, right down to his pencil-thin mustache. He came in and sat in the second pew. I could tell by the puzzled glances that the whole congregation wondered who he was.

I'm sure Mama played offertory music that night, but all I could hear was the thud of the coins as they dropped into the tambourine. I slowly worked my way around the room toward the elegant stranger until finally I stood directly in front of him.

A hint of a smile played around his lips. He reached into his jacket pocket, pulled out a cloth napkin, and slipped it onto the tambourine. It was so heavy that I had to steady the tambourine with both hands. "Thank you!" I croaked as I watched twenty silver dollars roll out of the napkin.

Returning to the front of the church, I could not contain my happiness. Mama was staring at me curiously. I pointed to the tambourine and mouthed turkey. She didn't look surprised; she just smiled and launched into a rousing rendition of "When the Saints Go Marching In."

The stranger slipped out before the service ended, before anyone could ask who had sent him. I didn't have to ask. I knew. The next evening as Papa asked the blessing for our Thanksgiving feast I silently added a prayer of my own: Thank You, God, for always being faithful. From now on I'll try to be too. Mama's turkey and dressing had never tasted better.

Mama is in heaven now. I am the pastor of Papa's church. We have grown to more than one thousand members and have a beautiful new church building only three blocks from that two-bedroom house. I still sometimes worry about how our needs will be met, especially since my wife and I have three teenage sons. Then I hear Mama's whisper in my ear, "Don't worry, mijo. The Lord will provide." And He does. Not always as dramatically as that long-ago Thanksgiving eve, but just as surely.

CHRISTMAS LOAVES AND FISHES

RAYNIER MAHARAJ

On Christmas Eve in homes everywhere, there is quiet excitement. The festive feeling and the warmth of having family near brings to mind a Christmas tale I love to relate each year. It's a true story, even though it might sound unbelievable. And it gives proof that miracles do happen.

A long time ago there was a group of young people who decided to spread some Christmas cheer. They had discovered that there were several children who would be spending the festive day in a community hospital nearby. So they bought nice presents, wrapped them and, with guitars, sweet voices and one of the friends dressed as Santa Claus, dropped in unexpectedly at the hospital on Christmas Eve.

The children were overjoyed at seeing Santa, and by the time the group was finished handing out presents and singing Christmas carols, there were tears in everyone's eyes. From then on, it was decided they would play Santa every year.

The following Christmas Eve, the ladies at the hospital were included in the rounds, and by the third year it was expanded to embrace some poor children in the neighborhood.

On the fourth Christmas Eve, however, after all the rounds were made, Santa Claus looked into his bag and discovered there were a few extra toys left. So the friends mulled it over, trying to figure out what to do with them. Somebody mentioned that there were a few squatters' shacks nearby in which a couple of desperately poor families lived.

So the group decided to go there, thinking there were perhaps three families at most. But as they drove over the crest of the hill into this lonely area—it was around midnight now—the shocked group saw a number of people standing at the side of the street.

They were children—more than thirty of them. Behind them were not three shacks but rows and rows of shabby squatters' dwellings. As the cars drew to a stop, the children came running up, shouting with joy. It turned out they had been waiting patiently all night for Santa Claus. Somebody—no one could remember who—had told them he was coming, although *our* Santa had decided to go there only moments before.

Everyone was stunned, except for Santa. He was in a panic. He knew he didn't have enough toys for all these kids. Eventually, not wanting to disappoint the children, he decided to give whatever toys he had only to the smallest children. When the presents ran out, he'd just have to explain to the bigger kids what had happened.

So moments later he found himself perched on top of a car's hood as these thirty or more sparkling clean children, dressed in their best clothes, lined up in order of height, with the smallest first, for their moment with him. As each anxious child approached, Santa dipped into his bag, his heart heavy with dread, hoping to find at least one more toy. And, by some miracle, he found one each time he dipped. And as the last of the children received a present, Santa looked into his now deflated bag. It was empty—empty as it should have been twenty-four children ago.

With relief, he let out a hearty "Ho ho ho" and bade the kids farewell. But as he was about to enter the car (the reindeer, apparently had the day off), he heard a child scream, "Santa! Santa! Wait!" And out of the bushes rushed two little children, a boy and a girl. They had been asleep.

Santa's heart sank. This time he knew for sure he had no more toys. The bag was empty. But as the out-of-breath kids approached, he summoned up some courage and dipped into the bag once more. And, lo and behold, there were two more presents in there.

The group of friends, now all grown adults, still talk about this miracle on Christmas morning. They still have no explanation for it, other than the fact that it happened. How do I know so much about this? Well, I was the one playing Santa.

Chapter 4   God Heals My Hurts

Jarius was desperate: His daughter was dying, and he had run out of options. When Jesus arrived in the area, Jarius battled the crowds to get close to Him. He fell to his feet, pleading, "My little daughter is dying. Please come and put your hands on her so that she will be healed and live." Jesus agreed and off they headed, toward Jarius's house and sick child. On the way, the crowds pushed and tugged at Jesus until one woman, also desperate for healing, darted in to touch His cloak. Jesus stopped, determined to figure out who had done this, losing vital time. Jarius must have been frantic with worry and anxiety.

But before they could start off again, some of Jarius's colleagues appeared with the worst news: "Your daughter is dead," they said. "Why bother the teacher any more?" Jesus ignored the friends, reassuring Jarius, "Don't be afraid; just believe." With Peter, James and John in tow, Jesus followed Jarius home, where the professional mourners were already wailing their grief. After silencing them, Jesus boldly told them, "The child is not dead. She's asleep." The wails turned into laughs of ridicule, and Jesus pushed them out of the house. Then with Jarius and his wife and the disciples, Jesus went to the girl, held her hand and told her, "Little girl, I say to you, get up!" And she did.

Everyone was astonished, naturally, not the least of whom was that little girl. Jesus was careful to instruct her parents to give her something to eat. What a wonderful meal that must have been!

For this child and her parents, there was no doubt about God's love and goodness. There was no doubt about the truth of Jesus' words. And for all her days, this little girl was a witness to her family and her community that God heals our hurts.

Heal me, O LORD, and I will be healed;
save me and I will be saved,
for you are the one I praise.

—Jeremiah 17:14

THE GARDENER

DONNA MCDONNALL

My son Danny's passion for archery started when he was nine. He came home from his 4-H group one summer day, all excited. "Guess what I did," he said. "Shot a bow and arrow like Robin Hood!" He was hooked. He used his older brother David's long bow until we bought him his own for Christmas. Danny practiced on a target in our backyard sometimes for two hours a day and entered local contests. But by the following summer, he was complaining about a persistent pain in his right shoulder. "Maybe you're practicing too much," I said. "Go easy on yourself." When the pain didn't let up, I took him to our pediatrician, and then to an orthopedist. We were referred to Dr. Ross Wilkins, an orthopedic surgeon in Denver.

Over dinner one night, my husband Bruce and I planned the four-hour trip to Denver. Danny seemed subdued. "What's wrong, honey?" I asked. Rubbing his shoulder, Danny looked at me. "Am I gonna be able to use my bow and arrow again soon, Mom?"

"Of course, Danny. Of course you will," I said, trying to sound convincing. But how could I know for sure?

"Don't worry, you guys," Bruce said. "Everything will be okay." Still, I could hear the concern in his voice, too.

Later that week after Dr. Wilkins examined Danny, he asked to speak to Bruce and me alone in his office.

"Danny has a form of bone cancer called Ewing's sarcoma," Dr. Wilkins said. "His arm hurts because he has a tumor growing on his right shoulder blade. We hope to be able to save Danny's arm with a new surgical technique. Of course, the main objective is to save his life."

Bruce squeezed my hand. "What's next?" he asked.

"Three months of chemotherapy first. We want to kill as many of the cancer cells as possible and reduce the size of that tumor. If the chemo works, Danny won't lose his arm. I'll remove his right shoulder blade instead, and whatever tumor remains." I turned to Bruce, but Dr. Wilkins wasn't finished. "Then we'll follow up with eighteen months more chemotherapy after Danny recovers from the surgery."

"He loves his archery," I said. "Danny will want to know if he'll ever be able to shoot his bow and arrow again."

"Let's take one step at a time," Dr. Wilkins replied.

On the way back home to Lamar, Bruce and I explained everything to Danny, except the chance of losing his arm. "I'll be okay," he said confidently. "But I guess I won't be able to shoot my arrows for a while." I turned my head so he wouldn't see my tears. *Lord, how can I tell him he might never be able to pick up a bow and arrow again?*

At home we talked to David, age thirteen, and eight-year-old Sara. "Is Danny going to be okay, Mommy?" Sara asked.

"Of course he's gonna be okay," David said. "He's my brother!"

The summer passed in a blur. Friends looked after David and Sara while Bruce and I drove Danny to Denver for overnight stays at the hospital every other week. Danny remained calm and good-natured, even when he was sick from the chemotherapy.

"I don't know where he gets his strength," Ramona, my church friend, commented.

"Danny is in God's hands," I said, trying to reassure myself as well.

After Danny underwent an MRI and CAT scan near the end of September, Dr. Wilkins called us at home. "Good news," he said. "The tumor's size was reduced, so I'm hopeful about keeping Danny's arm. I'd like to get him in here for surgery next week."

Dr. Wilkins explained his plan: After removing the shoulder blade, he'd use an Achilles tendon from the bone and tissue bank, and connect it to Danny's collarbone, shoulder muscle and upper arm bone. Danny would wear a sling until the tendon was fully reattached and stronger. "We won't know how much movement Danny will have in his arm until he's had months of physical therapy," Dr. Wilkins said. "There is no guarantee. As far as I know, I'll be the first to try this surgery."

Friends said they'd take care of David and Sara, and Ramona promised, "I have everybody at church praying for Danny."

In Denver, Bruce and I checked into the Ronald McDonald House, then brought Danny to the hospital to get ready for surgery. I kissed him and gave him a big hug. "We'll see you soon, Danny."

He smiled. "I'll be okay, Mom," he said. "See you soon, Dad."

Six hours later Dr. Wilkins emerged from the operating room. "We were able to save Danny's arm," he said. "The surgery went perfectly. Danny's a strong boy."

As soon as Danny was allowed visitors, our friends brought David and Sara. "I want everybody to sign my sling," Danny said. *How can he be so cheerful?* I wondered, staring at the thin, wispy hair on his head.

"We miss you a lot," Sara said, kissing Danny right on his bald spot.

"We'll be horsing around again in no time," David said.

After a couple of hours, it was time for the kids to leave. Bruce saw them out, and I pulled my chair next to Danny's bed.

"I can't wait to go home, Mom," he said. "I want to start practicing with my bow and arrow."

Taking Danny's hand, I looked him in the eye. "Danny, that might be a long, long time from now."

He stared at me determinedly. "I'm gonna get better, Mom. I just know it! And I'll be an archer again! You'll see."

Dr. Wilkins came in later that day with more good news. "I'll discharge Danny if you two can stick around Denver for a few days so we can monitor his progress." Danny was thrilled, and my friend Ramona made things even better. Her parents lived in Denver and were on vacation. "Why don't you and Danny stay at the house?" she offered.

Danny and I moved in. There was a big garden out back. We spent our first night eating popcorn in front of the TV. But the next day Danny seemed down.

"Want some ice cream?" I asked. He followed me into the kitchen, where I got out bowls and spoons.

"Mom," he said tentatively.

"Yes, Danny?" I said, scooping the ice cream.

"How long will it be until I can shoot my bow and arrow again? Tell me the truth."

I put his bowl in front of him. "It'll be a while before we know, Danny," I said. It was the first time I'd heard him express doubt. He mixed his ice cream around in the bowl and pushed it away. "What if the next round of chemotherapy doesn't work?" he asked.

"Danny," I said, putting my arms around him, "we just have to trust the Lord." I didn't know what more I could do to help my son.

When I went to put the ice cream back in the freezer I glanced out the sliding glass doors into the garden. A man in overalls was coming up the walk. He was carrying a rake. He tapped on the glass. "Hello, there," he said when I slid the door open. "Name's Gus. I'm taking care of the garden while the folks are away."

"I'm Donna," I said, "and this is my son, Danny. We're just staying the week."

The man hitched his overalls up and looked at Danny kindly. "What happened to your arm, soldier?" he asked.

"Danny had surgery to remove a tumor from his shoulder blade," I explained.

The man nodded. "Same thing happened to me when I was young," he said. "Here, look at this." He turned around. "Shoulder blade's gone. Doctors said I might not have much movement again, but look." He stepped back and swung his arm around, letting the rake rest on his shoulder. "I can do anything I want. Don't you worry, son," he said. "You will be able to do whatever you want too." Danny's face brightened.

"Well," the man said, "I'll be on my way. Just keep working at it, son. You'll be good as new." I closed the door, and Danny dug into his ice cream.

"That man was nice," I said.

Danny looked up from his bowl. "He sure was!"

Danny was soon his cheerful self again, and his attitude rubbed off on me. That visit from the gardener was just what we needed to get us both thinking straight again. As Dr. Wilkins had said, we'd take this one step at a time.

When Ramona's parents returned, I asked them about Gus. "Who?" they said. "We didn't ask anyone to watch our garden."

I tried again: "Maybe it was one of the neighbors."

Ramona's mom shook her head. "We don't know anyone named Gus," she said. "I can't imagine who that could've been."

I thought about the gardener's visit some more, and I realized that Gus said he'd had the same operation when he was a young man. That would have been many years ago. How can that be possible? I wondered. Danny's surgery had been the first of its kind—based on Dr. Wilkins's groundbreaking studies. Had God sent the gardener to help my son in a way neither I nor the doctors could?

We returned home to Lamar, and Danny started physical therapy once a week. "I plan to shoot my bow and arrow again," Danny announced at his first session.

"Danny . . ." I began.

"It's okay," the therapist said. "We can tailor Danny's exercises to help him do that." Danny beamed. Every three weeks we went to Denver for chemotherapy treatments. A year and a half after his surgery, Danny was shooting his bow and arrow.

Today, twelve years later, Danny is cancer-free and his target practice is right on. He will graduate from college with a double major in biochemistry and neurobiology, and has already worked at Dr. Wilkins's limb-preservation institute, helping with research. Danny is debating between graduate and medical schools, and looks forward to a career in medicine. Incidentally, Danny's also taken an interest in gardening.

"WHAT DID SHE PUT ON MY SISTER'S FACE?"

JACKIE, AS TOLD TO CHARLIE W. SHEDD

We were camping at a state park in Tennessee. We are a close family and we do this every summer. My father is an insurance salesman and my mother a schoolteacher. There are five of us with my two sisters and me.

My father was grilling hamburgers when all of a sudden my little sister came running down the road, screaming. Blood was all over her face because she was cut just awful. When she ran up to us we could tell she'd fallen into some glass. Some of the glass was still sticking from her face and her hands. You could tell it hurt a lot.

My father ran to the park office to ask for help. But they told him the nearest hospital was twelve miles away. She was bleeding so much, we had to do something right away. By now lots of campers were coming to see what was wrong, but nobody knew what to do. Then from nowhere a tall lady came right up to us and offered to help, "I have some salve I can put on her face to make her stop bleeding. It will also keep her from hurting anymore."

She was tall and kind of thin, but not too thin. She was a beautiful lady with very dark hair and dark skin too. She also had a beautiful smile and there was something about her eyes, something that made us believe she knew what she was doing and she could really help my sister.

Well, what would you do? My folks decided they would let the lady go ahead. Someone stretched a blanket on the picnic table and put my sister on it. Then the lady took what looked like thick dark chocolate and rubbed it all over my sister's face and hands. The dark lady hardly said anything at all but all the time she was putting the stuff of my sister's face she kept singing soft and low. My sister quit crying right away and after a little while she went to sleep.

Of course all of us were looking at my sister because we were amazed at how quickly her bleeding stopped. Nobody saw the lady slip away. She was gone before we could thank her or find out what the salve was.

My sister slept all night and in the morning she was fine. There was no glass sticking in her skin and we could hardly tell where she had been cut. And she never got any scars. Not one.

All this was four years ago and we don't know what really happened any more now than we did then. Of course we talk about it a lot and one of the things we always ask is something you probably would ask too: *"Was the lady with the salve an angel?"*

My father and mother and all of us are really religious people. Like I said, my father is an insurance salesman but in our church he is also what is called a lay preacher. I have heard him talk about the lady and my sister many times. He always asks, "Do you think that lady was an angel? Well, there must have been an angel somewhere. If your child was healed overnight, I think you might pray this same prayer we pray real often in our family devotions. 'Thank You, God, for Your angels.'"

ANNA'S CURE

REBEKAH MONTGOMERY

Early August 1994

As a mother, Jenny Miller couldn't quiet the nagging feeling that something was very seriously wrong with three-year-old Anna, the next to the youngest of her five children.

"I had taken her to the pediatrician several times, and each time he said she was fine. But it wasn't just her thin arms that made me think she was sick," said Jenny. "When I would give her a piece of candy, she wouldn't eat it. She'd put it in her pocket, and I knew there was something wrong with that!"

October 13, 1994

As evening fell, Jenny attempted to stifle her fears for Anna.

Earlier that day, Jenny had again taken Anna to the pediatrician. He had looked at her distended abdomen and skinny arms, but once more he pronounced her healthy. He thought that perhaps she might have a kidney infection or bronchitis.

But Anna was so weak she could barely walk. Her stomach didn't seem merely pudgy to Jenny, it seemed swollen; and Anna was coughing so hard she had trouble catching her breath. Jenny wondered if the child would live through the night.

In desperation, Jenny took Anna to the home of a physician friend from their church. When he examined the gravely ill child, he shared Jenny's concern.

"As a doctor, I can't tell you that your pediatrician is all wrong," he said cautiously, unwilling to criticize another physician. Then he gave Jenny the name of a different doctor and urged her to take Anna to see him in the morning.

The remainder of the evening was a nightmare for both mother and daughter.

"I propped Anna up on the couch, but she could hardly breathe. I saw fear in her eyes," said Jenny. That fear matched the terror in Jenny's own heart.

The next afternoon, the new doctor temporarily put Jenny's mind at ease; however, he admitted Anna to the university hospital for tests and observation. Jenny went home to care for her other children while her husband J.P. stayed by Anna's side.

By 10:00 P.M., their newfound confidence was severely shaken by the results of a CAT scan.

"It might be cancer," J.P. told Jenny over the phone. "They've put chest tubes in because she is drowning in fluid."

As quickly as she could, Jenny drove back to the hospital. Attached to all kinds of tubes and machinery, Anna looked small and pale and vulnerable.

"I wanted to scoop her up and run out of the hospital," Jenny said later, but she knew she could not shield her beloved child from an uncertain future or protect her from the terrible disease that lurked inside her tiny body.

Jenny and J.P. held one another and prayed for their small daughter. "God, Anna is Yours. You can heal her or You can take her home. You know what is best."

"At that moment," said Jenny later, "I realized that she was in God's arms—and anything was possible with God."

Over the next weeks God continually gave Jenny confirmation that He was holding Anna in his arms. Card after card came with Isaiah 40:11 on it: "He tends his flock like a shepherd: He gathers the lambs in his arms and carries them close to his heart; he gently leads those that have young."

Still, the night was very dark for Jenny. Uncertain what diagnosis tomorrow would bring, she and J.P. went home to their other children and spent a sleepless night. Jenny lay in bed dreading the dawn, and when it finally came, she told J.P., "It's so hard to face today. I want to just stay in bed."

J.P. quietly told her, "Anna has to face the day."

"It put everything back into perspective for me," Jenny said. "I thought, *This might be hard for me, but it will really be hard for Anna.*"

Worse moments were yet to come.

Back at the hospital that morning, Jenny and J.P. sat down with the doctors who told them the awful truth: Anna had stage four of a form of cancer called neuroblastoma. Her tumor was the largest of this type that the hospital doctors had ever seen and was very progressed.

"What is beyond stage four?" Jenny asked.

The doctor was brutally honest. "Death," he said. "She has less than a five percent chance of survival." But the doctor went on to outline a rigorous regime of chemotherapy and radiation.

Knowing how difficult chemotherapy could be, J.P. asked, "Is this prolonging something that's going to happen anyway? Is there a light at the end of the tunnel?"

"There is a light," said the doctor, "but it's a very small light and it's very far away."

As long as there was a chance, Jenny and J.P. decided not to give up. "We'll go ahead with the treatment plan and see what happens," they told the doctor.

Although she was in the intensive care unit for the next six weeks, Anna immediately started radiation and the first of eight courses of chemotherapy. After that, she was in and out of the hospital so much that the Millers' four other children—all home-schooled—went intermittently to stay with their grandparents in Indiana.

March 1995

It was a quiet time at the Miller house, too quiet for Jenny. Her other children were with their grandparents and only a gravely ill Anna was in the house.

"I had been praying that God would give us some hope for the future," said Jenny. "I was praying that life could get back to normal." But even Jenny was surprised how God supplied that hope.

While she was holding Anna on the couch, Anna said to her, "Mom, you got a baby in your tummy."

Jenny and J.P. were shocked at the child's matter-of-fact announcement.

"How do you know?" they asked Anna.

"God told me," said Anna. "He stood by my bed in the hospital and said, 'Your mommy's got a baby in her tummy.'"

Although Jenny had no suspicions that she was pregnant, the next day she conducted a home pregnancy test. It was positive.

Jenny was apprehensive.

"I was anxious about having a new baby on top of my responsibilities for Anna and the other kids," she said.

But shortly thereafter, J.P. and Anna were looking at a Bible picture book together.

"Daddy, that's what I saw!" Anna pointed at a picture of Christ. "Jesus in the sun! He said, 'Don't be afraid. You're not gonna die!'"

Jenny said she then realized God had given comforting knowledge to Anna—and He had sent a message for her, as well.

"It brought me peace that this was a sign from God. It was as if He was saying, 'You don't have to worry about November when the baby is due. Everything is going to be okay.'"

There was a great outpouring of love and prayers for Anna and the entire Miller family. "People at the grocery store would tell me that they were praying for Anna every day," said Jenny.

Then in June 1995, with a flood of prayer support, Anna had a stem cell transplant. She recovered and was able to go home in only three weeks' time, a record for a transplant recovery.

Anna began to regain her strength with amazing speed. She did well until October 1995. Two weeks before Jenny was due to deliver the new baby, Anna was stricken with shingles, a typical malady for a stem cell transplant patient. But she made a complete recovery, although her eyes remained sensitive to light. This was the last time Anna was hospitalized.

Jenny's son Avery was born November 6, 1995.

Postscript

Anna's life is a witness to the healing power of Christ. As a result of Anna's illness, combined with the witness of other believers, the doctor who diagnosed Anna's cancer came to commit his life to Christ.

At Anna's last follow-up CAT scan in December 1998, Jenny overheard a substitute doctor handling Anna's treatment remark to one of the nurses, "Boy, she is a real miracle! It's a miracle that she made it!"

Anna has had no recurrence of the cancer. If this continues, she will be considered cancer-free in another year. Anna has remained friendly with many of the nurses, but she remembers little of her ordeal.

THE HEALING

SANDY JONES

The shock of events of the past thirty hours overwhelmed Jim all at once. His body felt numb, and while the world was moving along, he felt removed from it.

Jim and his wife Connie had just lost their beautiful four-month-old son. Preliminary diagnosis: SIDS, sudden infant death syndrome.

Thirty hours ago Jim had driven to the baby-sitter's home to pick up Joshua. It was a routine trip, like the one he made five days every week . . . until he arrived, and little Joshua could not be awakened from his nap. The next few hours were a blur. Wailing sirens, swift-moving paramedics, critical-care doctors and reassuring nurses, holding hands and praying. A decision to life-flight Joshua to Children's Hospital sixty miles away . . . but all in vain. Twelve hours later, the doctors had exhausted all attempts at revival. There was no brain activity. The decision was to turn off life-support. Little Joshua was gone. Yes, they wanted all of Joshua's usable organs to be readied for donation. That was not a difficult decision for Jim and Connie, a loving and giving couple.

The next morning dawned. More decisions and arrangements. Telephone calls and funeral plans. At one point Jim realized he needed a haircut, but being new to the community, he didn't have his own regular barber yet. Jim's brother volunteered to call his hairdresser and get Jim an appointment. The schedule was full. But after a few words of explanation, the salon owner said, "Just send him right over and we'll take care of him."

Jim was exhausted as he settled into the chair. He had had little sleep. He began to reflect on the past hours, trying desperately to make some sense of it all. Why had Joshua, their firstborn, the child for whom they had waited so long, been taken so soon . . . he had barely begun his life. . . . The question kept coming, and the pain in Jim's heart just enveloped him. He thought about the words spoken by the hospital chaplain. "We don't fully understand what part we have in God's plan. Perhaps Joshua had already completed his mission on earth." Those words didn't ease the bitterness that was creeping in.

The hairdresser expressed her sympathy, and Jim found himself telling her all about the events of the last thirty hours. Somehow it helped to tell the story. Maybe if he told it enough times, he would gain some understanding.

As Jim mentioned the organ donations, he looked at his watch and remembered what was happening sixty miles away . . . where he had said good-bye to his beloved Joshua a few short hours earlier. "They are transplanting one of his heart valves right now."

The hairdresser stopped and stood motionless. Finally she spoke, but her voice quivered and it was only a whisper. "You're not going to believe this . . . but about an hour ago the customer sitting in this chair wanted me to hurry so she could get to Children's Hospital. She left here so full of joy . . . her prayers had been answered. Today her baby granddaughter is receiving a desperately needed transplant . . . a heart valve."

Jim's healing began.

THE TRUE THANKSGIVING

JOAN WESTER ANDERSON

It was Thanksgiving 1988. Jane and Alban Theriault's children and grandchildren were at their house in Lewiston, Maine, to celebrate—in both French and English (the family has always been bilingual). Alban lifted the huge turkey out of the oven, set it on the countertop and loaded the baster with drippings for a final squirt.

Just then, the Theriaults' nine-year-old granddaughter Kari skipped up. "Pepere, can I help?" she asked.

"Be careful, dear," Alban began, but to his horror, the boiling-hot fat spurted out of the dropper in his hand and splashed over Kari's face. "Oh no!" he shouted as the little girl screamed in pain. People came running from every room.

Kari was badly burned. Gravy drippings had splattered on her chin and half of her mouth, and had scalded her tongue. Liquid had also fallen on her chest, and since her dress was made of nylon, the high heat had burned even more deeply.

Kari's mother Christine, a nurse, decided not to take her hysterical daughter to the hospital. She did everything for Kari that the emergency-room staff would have done, then put her in Alban and Jane's bed.

"Kari cried for four hours," Jane recalls. "Her skin split open and hung from her chin. The blotches on her chest were raw. It was the worst Thanksgiving—the worst day—any of us had ever had."

Perhaps Alban was the most devastated. How had he allowed this to happen? Kari would be scarred for life—and every time she looked in the mirror, she would blame her grandfather. It was almost more than this quiet, gentle man could bear.

On Friday and Saturday, Kari's pain increased. Her tongue was badly burned, and her lips stuck together. Liquids from a straw were her only nourishment. Her face got worse and worse. Jane and Alban had four tickets for Father Ralph DiOrio's healing service on Sunday in Worcester. "Why don't we take Kari so Father can pray over her?" Jane suggested. Christine agreed.

There are usually thousands of people at this kind of service, and crowd control is imperative. "No one can get to Father DiOrio unless *he* calls *you*," Jane explains. But Jane couldn't wait for that. When the priest left the stage to bless people in the balcony, Jane grasped Kari's hand, went to the opposite end of the hall, outside and around the building, then inside, right where Father DiOrio was approaching.

An usher came up, presumably to tell Jane she was blocking the aisle and would have to leave. "But I could hear Father making his way through the crowds, and as he came down some stairs, I turned Kari around toward him," she recalls.

Father DiOrio stopped. "What happened to her?" he asked Jane.

"She's been burned with hot gravy, Father."

The priest took holy oil from his pocket, touched Kari's wounds with it, and prayed for her healing. Jane began to thank God. She felt certain that everything would be all right.

The next morning when Kari awakened, she said, "I'm hungry, Mom. Can I have some real food?"

Christine looked at her. Her raw face and chest didn't seem any better. "Kari, you know you can't eat," she reminded her.

"Mom, I'm fine. Nothing hurts, really."

Kari did eat an enormous breakfast, so Christine agreed to send her to school. Kari's teacher and classmates were horrified at her injuries, and she spent all day explaining what had happened. But on Tuesday, oddly, the wounds seemed to be closing. On Thursday when Kari got up, her mother screamed. "Kari! Look in the mirror!"

Kari did. Neither of them could believe what they saw. Kari's skin was smooth and perfect. Not a scar, not even a blister remained to show where the sores had been. Her teacher and friends were astonished too. How could such terrible wounds simply vanish?

Alban Theriault took Kari with him to prayer meeting that week. He held her high in his arms, tears of joy spilling down his cheeks, his broken heart mended. And Jane, too, pondered this wonderful occurrence. "It was interesting that we just 'happened' to have four tickets for the healing service," she muses. "And even more interesting that God took away Kari's pain first, but not her burns—which allowed her to go to school, where many witnessed the damage."

Days later, everyone saw a little girl's perfectly restored face—and knew what God had done.

Chapter 5   God Is Generous with His Miracles

Sometimes it's just a matter of being in the right place at the right time—with the right attitude. John's telling of the story of Jesus feeding the multitudes includes details missing in other accounts. Most notably, in this account we meet a little boy with a lunch of two fish and five small barley loaves. Andrew presents this child with his stash of food to Jesus as a meager offering toward the sea of hunger surging around them.

Jesus took that little boy's lunch, blessed it and began distributing it to the five thousand men (the women and children would have added to that count!) seated on the grass. Everyone ate as much as they wanted, and the disciples gathered up twelve full baskets of leftover bread.

Each account of feeding a multitude of people speaks not only to God's concern for our physical needs, but to His bountiful generosity. In each account Jesus is surrounded by hungry, restless people who have been listening to His teachings and following Him around. Jesus begins with a small helping of food, he blesses it, and begins to break off pieces and pass them out to the hungry. And after everyone is satisfied, the disciples pick up the leftovers.

But John's account includes a generous child, perhaps even one of those children that the disciples would have tried to keep away from Jesus. Jesus took the gift of this child, this modest lunch, and transformed it into a celebration of God's unrivaled generosity. Multiplication miracles reflect God's bountiful love and His eagerness to use our small offerings as a starting point that expands and expands until all of His children are fed and satisfied.

That little boy had a story to tell his mother that night, and without a doubt, he never tasted anything as sweet and satisfying as that meal served by Jesus. This little boy discovered firsthand that God is generous with His miracles.

I will praise you, O Lord, with all my heart;
I will tell of all your wonders.
I will be glad and rejoice in you;
I will sing praise to your name, O Most High.

—Psalm 9:1–2

FOR LOVE OF LOGAN

JOAN WESTER ANDERSON

Tami Carroll grew up in a small Indiana town, married in 1986 shortly after her high school graduation and had her first baby, Jaclyn, a few years later. "It was a routine pregnancy and delivery, no trouble at all," Tami recalls. She and husband Todd settled into a peaceful life on their farm, enjoying parenthood and planning a larger family. There was no warning of what was to come.

Tami became pregnant again in 1993. Everything seemed normal until her sixth month, when an ultrasound revealed problems. Tami's obstetrician, Dr. Diana Okon, gently broke the news. "The baby had chromosomal abnormalities, stemming from a condition that is always fatal," Dr. Okon says. The child, a girl, would die either during the next few months or shortly after birth.

Tami and Todd were heartbroken. They named their unborn daughter Megan, and hoped she knew how much they loved her. Eventually Tami gave birth, but there was little to celebrate, for baby Megan was stillborn. "My mother had died when I was twenty," Tami said, "and at the time I thought there could be no greater pain than losing a parent. But now I had to admit that the pain of losing a child was even worse." Also difficult was the seed of doubt that had been planted. Could this happen again—did the Carrolls have some kind of genetic defect? Worse, what if Megan was the last child they would ever conceive?

Tests on Tami and Todd showed nothing amiss, however, and eventually Tami became pregnant again. But now she was nervous, afraid to get her hopes up. In addition, although Tami had grown up as a Southern Baptist, she hadn't been to church in years. "For some reason, I had sort of given up on God," she admits. "At times, I felt that even if He was listening to me, He probably didn't care." But gradually, as this pregnancy progressed, Tami found herself talking to her Heavenly Father. "God, please give me a healthy baby," she asked each day, Megan's death still fresh in her mind. Even if she and God had not been close for a while, He surely wouldn't ask her to go through another loss like that, would He?

Time passed, and despite her worry, Tami had no problems. Dr. Okon monitored her carefully, doing a chromosomal test as well as extra ultrasounds. The baby—a boy whom the Carrolls had already named Logan—looked vital and completely normal.

Tami was due on April 9, 1995. But when she went to the office for her scheduled checkup on April 5, Dr. Okon decided to hospitalize her early the next morning. "I think she knew I was worried, and it might be better for me to be induced in a controlled setting," Tami explains.

The following morning, Todd and Tami drove to Clarke Memorial Hospital in nearby Jeffersonville. Tami was admitted, labor began, and everything seemed fine. Baby Logan was closely monitored, and his heart was healthy and strong. Todd and Ruthie, Tami's sister, were with her, and as things progressed, the grandparents assembled in the waiting room. It would be a joyous event—not like the last time, they all assured each other. New life was budding. Logan was almost here!

By late afternoon, Dr. Okon had delivered two other babies, and was as ready as Tami to meet little Logan. Her contractions strong and healthy, Tami was taken to the delivery room. She was almost to the end now, and as the nurses cheered her on, she pushed and pushed. "One more!" a nurse shouted. "He's almost here!" Tami pushed again. But Logan's heart rate had suddenly slowed. And at 4:42 P.M., as Dr. Okon took him from the womb, there was no heartbeat at all. "There was a loose umbilical cord around the infant's neck that slid off easily. . . . [His] mouth and nose were bulb-suctioned on the perineum and the fluid was clear," Dr. Okon wrote in a later report. But the baby's Apgar score—the test that determines newborn health—was zero. He wasn't breathing.

"Call code," Dr. Okon quickly told a nurse as she carried the lifeless infant to the warmer on the other side of the room, and gave him oxygen. "Come on, Logan!" she murmured. "Wake up . . . " Another nurse started chest compressions.

There was no cry, no heartbeat or pulse. The baby's eyes remained closed, his limbs limp, his color an unhealthy gray.

"Logan?" Tami asked. "Todd, why isn't he crying?"

Todd stood in shock, watching nurses running here and there. No one was saying anything, and the silence was horrible. *Logan, Logan, please cry.* . . . Ruthie realized something terrible was happening, and hurriedly left the room.

Within seconds, it seemed, an emergency room physician raced in, followed by Tami's pediatrician, who had been summoned from her nearby office. One of the nurses phoned Kosair Children's Hospital in nearby Louisville, Kentucky, which has a neonatal unit and specialists on call. A respiratory therapist passed Tami, then an X-ray technician. "What is going on?" Tami screamed, beginning to sob. Tears streamed down Todd's cheeks.

A nurse tried to comfort them. "We don't know anything yet," she whispered.

It couldn't be happening, not again. She couldn't lose another child . . . *Logan, please breathe.*

Dr. Okon came to Tami's side, to finish the delivery process. The specialists, she explained softly, had intubated the baby and were forcing air into his lungs. Someone had injected medication, someone else was taking X-rays, everything possible was being done. . . . To Tami, it was all a horrible nightmare. She had thought everything was under control, and now she realized that nothing was. Only God could help Logan now. "Dear God," she whispered through her tears, "please don't do this. I don't think I can handle it. Please save Logan, please."

Medical personnel continued to work over the baby. "But Logan never showed any signs of life, nor did he respond to any of the advanced cardiac life support efforts by the code team," says Dr. Okon. At 5:15, thirty-five minutes after delivery, the neonatal specialists from Kosair and Clarke hospital personnel agreed to discontinue all resuscitation efforts. Logan was pronounced dead.

Unobtrusively, a nurse baptized Logan. Another weighed him—eight pounds, three ounces—cleaned him, wrapped him in warm blankets, put a little stocking cap on his dark head and laid him in Tami's arms for a last good-bye. She held him close, searching his perfect little face. "Logan, don't go—I need you," she whispered. But her son's eyes were closed, his body completely limp. *Dear God, please* . . . she had to let go, to accept the inevitable, but somehow, she couldn't stop praying.

Dr. Okon and the pediatrician stood by Tami's bed; the others had left the delivery room. "We don't know what happened, Tami," Dr. Okon said. "We won't have any answers unless we do an autopsy."

Tami blinked back tears. Perhaps an autopsy would save another family the suffering she was enduring. "All right," she agreed. "But I want to hold him for a while."

"Of course." Someone brought a consent form, and still holding Logan, Tami reached over and signed it. Dr. Okon left the room to break the news to the Carroll relatives in the waiting room; soon they streamed inn, murmuring words of encouragement, mingling their tears with Tami's and Todd's.

Todd cuddled Logan, then passed him to Ruthie. The nurse took some photographs. Occasionally the baby's body moved slightly, and the first time it happened, the nurse went out to the front desk and alerted Dr. Okon, who was talking to her partner on the phone. Dr. Okon explained that such a phenomenon was called "agonal breathing," and was just a spasm or a reaction to the medication the baby had received. How unfortunate, she thought, that the Carrolls had seen it—it was almost like Logan dying twice.

At 5:55 P.M., mourning was coming to an end, at least for the moment. It was time, everyone knew, to turn Logan's body over to the hospital. Tami's stepmother was holding him, and she bent over to say a last good-bye. Once again, his little body went into a spasm. Tami's stepmother looked and looked again. "Tami, he—he's gasping!" she cried. "Look, his leg moved!"

"It's just a spasm, like the nurse said," Tami answered.

"I don't think so—I think he's breathing," Grandma exclaimed. "Ruthie, get a nurse!"

Ruthie did. In an attempt to calm the family, the same nurse came quickly and put her fingertips on the baby's chest. Then she reached for a stethoscope and listened. "Wait right here!" she shouted, as she ran from the room.

Dr. Okon was still filling out forms when the excited nurse approached her. "She said, 'The Carroll baby has a heartbeat,' and I responded, 'The next one to have a heart attack is going to be me if this doesn't stop,'" Dr. Okon reports. But when she reached the now silent room and approached Tami's stepmother, she could see that the baby was turning pink. "He's alive?" she asked the older woman.

Tami's stepmother could only nod, her arms trembling. Astonished, Dr. Okon took the baby from her. His little chest was rising and falling rapidly. "He *is* alive!" she cried. "Let's take him to the nursery!" Nurse and physician ran with the infant out of the room.

Tami began to weep. She had been grieving for over an hour for her child, and now, it seemed, the cycle had started over. "Don't do this again—I can't lose him twice!" she wept, as Todd, still thunderstruck, tried to comfort her.

"We don't know what's going on, Tami," he explained.

Tami did. It was just a cruel joke. For some reason Logan's little body was still reacting to treatment, and everyone thought . . . but such things were impossible! Her son had been dead for an hour and eighteen minutes—no one could come back to life after all that time.

And yet, she had asked God for a miracle, hadn't she?

Medical personnel began reappearing in the delivery room with bulletins for Tami and Todd. The neonatalists from Kosair Children's Hospital had returned, dumbfounded. They were currently examining Logan in the nursery. His disbelieving pediatrician was also there, along with doctors from all over the hospital, responding to the quickly spreading news. Despite the impossibility of it, Logan was breathing on his own, and appeared healthy. He had been placed in an oxygen tent, and tests were proceeding.

Of course, there were undertones that were not mentioned, at least not at this joyful, exultant moment. A baby clinically dead for over an hour would no doubt have severe brain damage, as well as nonfunctioning optic nerves, tissue damage, seizures—the list could be endless. But for now, everyone was in a state of awe. It was, as Dr. Okon described it later, like seeing the shadow of God passing by.

Baby Logan was transferred to Kosair Children's Hospital and remained there for five weeks. He slept for the first two, because of medication to reduce the possibility of seizures, then gradually began to awaken. Although brain-damaged babies often don't suck, he nursed immediately. Tests showed that his eyes and hearing were completely normal. Today he is progressing a bit more slowly than the average baby, but his neurologist is "cautiously optimistic" that Logan's future is bright.

What happened to this very special baby? No one really knows. So far, there has been no medical explanation, only theories suggesting that Logan may have experienced the same kind of situation as a drowning victim—when systems shut down for a time, then spontaneously revive. But Logan had never actually *been* alive after birth, and Dr. Okon, who has seen nothing like it in her years of practice, is grateful that she was not the only specialist on the scene. "If I had been alone," she told Tami, "I might have concluded that I had made a mistake, missed a tiny sign of life. But there were other physicians there, including neonatologists, and we all agreed." Logan was dead, and then he was resurrected.

The "how" is hard enough to answer, the "why" almost impossible. "While Logan was hospitalized, I saw other babies who were very sick," says Tami. "I remember thinking, *Why Logan? Why not these others?*"

Tami knows this answer will remain a mystery. But her baby's story has touched many—and perhaps that is a reason in itself. Medical personnel at Clarke Memorial Hospital have dubbed him "Lazarus." Strangers approach Tami on the street with tears in their eyes. Even an elderly lady wrote to tell the Carrolls that the same thing had happened to her at birth, and no one had ever believed her mother—until now. "Maybe God wanted to show us that miracles do happen, to say, 'I'm still here and I still raise people from the dead,'" Tami says. "And maybe it's not my job to ask *why*, but just to keep telling others, and keep saying thank you."

She and Todd are very willing to carry out that heavenly assignment. What else can one do with such a wonder?

THE MIRACLE BABY

JOHN HOLMSTROM

Janet and Bob Steele are married and live in Lake Elsinore, California. Janet, thirty-two years old, is a nurse and Bob, thirty-one, is a computer operator for a bank. Janet is short and sturdy and has a nurse's no-nonsense attitude towards life. Robert is a lanky, talkative, and thoughtful man who clearly enjoys fatherhood. Their sons are Joshua, age three, and Nathaniel, five months. While I was interviewing Bob and Janet, Joshua tried to include us all in his attempts to play with the cat while little Nathaniel lay quietly and happily in his father's arms. Janet and Bob took turns talking about the birth of Nathaniel.

JANET: At around four in the morning I went into labor. I told my husband and then got dressed and drove to the hospital. We decided my husband should stay with Joshua until someone could come over to watch him. As a nurse, I knew I could make the drive alone. It was no big deal since the birth of my first child had been no problem. I told Bob I'd call him when I got to the hospital.

I didn't realize there was a problem until I was actually in the examining room. When they monitored the baby's heart rate I could hear it and I knew it was bad. It was very slow, almost sluggish. The heart would stop and start. The nurses determined I had no amniotic fluid in my uterus, so they started rushing around to give me an amnio infusion, to get fluid around the baby.

I had worked at the hospital for nine years and all the nurses were my friends. They knew right away that I had to have an emergency Caesarean section, so they called the doctor and prepared themselves in case the doctor was late.

Everyone knew what to do and I was hoping they could perform the procedure in time. I don't recall anyone ever saying the baby was doing badly, it was an unspoken truth that they all knew. The Caesarean was going to be done right in the delivery room because they didn't have time to move me to an operating room. But while we were waiting for the anesthesiologist, the baby's heart rate picked up a little so they took me to the operating room.

Prior to the delivery, Bob and I had discussed having my tubes tied after the birth, but when the doctor arrived and realized what was happening, he recommended canceling the tubal ligation, "because this is an emergency and we don't know what's going to happen." In other words, I might want to have another baby so I shouldn't have my tubes tied. I agreed with him.

My background as a nurse in the delivery room helped me. I knew what everyone was doing and why. They didn't have to explain a lot to me. I just signed the papers and let them do the C-section. Getting emotional about it was not going to do anybody any good.

But it kept getting worse.

When they did the C-section they discovered the umbilical cord was wrapped around our baby's neck twice, very tightly. The doctor didn't know how long he had been without oxygen. Four minutes without oxygen can produce brain damage; it can start even sooner, depending on the trauma. The baby was limp with no muscle tone so they immediately gave him an IV into his umbilical cord. By now, an hour had passed since I arrived at the hospital.

Shortly thereafter, the baby started having seizures—usually an indication of brain damage. Cutting off oxygen to the brain causes lesions or scar tissue to form, and these, in turn, produce seizures. The doctor gave him dopamine to help his kidneys and his blood, phenobarbital for the seizures, and several other drugs. Still, his little arms were rigid, jerking and turning in, which is called posturing, and it's a sign of possible major brain damage.

After a C-section, a pediatrician always evaluates the condition of the baby on a scale of zero to nine. They consider muscle tone, breathing, response and so on. A normal baby is rated nine and nine. Nathaniel was two and four, which is very bad.

They gave him a two because he wasn't dead and because they had to give him some rating. I found out later he had the worst rating of any baby born that month. The night nursing supervisor called Bob and told him to come right away.

BOB: It was around five in the morning when the nurse called. My first reaction was total shock. As I drove to the hospital I kept thinking about "will"—God's will and my will. I prayed that God knew my heart and He knew that my will was to have a healthy baby. I prayed that He would keep me strong and help me accept whatever was His will.

When I got to the hospital, Janet was unconscious in the recovery room. At that point I was still in a state of shock—I didn't know what to think. I called one of the elders of our church and asked her if they would pray for our baby. We all prayed right away that God would heal him and give us the strength to deal with whatever came our way.

JANET: Bob was made aware of everything that was going on with Nathaniel while I was still unconscious from the anesthesia. There were two nursery nurses in attendance, and one was crying because she knew how bad it was. She wouldn't even go in the delivery room.

After I revived, Bob and I prayed together and separately. We had the church praying for us, his sister and her husband in Hawaii praying for us, as well as our relatives in Nebraska and Michigan. We had a real prayer chain in action.

BOB: When I first saw Nathaniel, he had an IV and a ventilator to help him breathe. He wasn't doing well. His whole body was shaking and his arms were flailing, like one continuous shiver. It was really weird because even though he looked bad, I was confident that God could make things all right. I felt God could do anything and since I had already asked Him for help, it wasn't logical to get angry or throw things. That would be assuming the worst.

I had my Bible with me and I read, mostly by myself. I read passages about how the Lord is your shepherd and He will provide, He is your comforter and will take care of you.

JANET: I was mostly praying, "Please, God, give me the strength to deal with this." We didn't know whether Nathaniel was going to live or die. And if he did live, we didn't know what kind of condition he would be in. If he wasn't going to be okay, I still wanted to love him, and if he died. . . .

Our community hospital is small and doesn't have a neonatal intensive care unit. I was able to see Nathaniel for only a few minutes before a doctor's assistant took him to the University of Irvine Hospital's intensive care unit about an hour away.

BOB: We can't understand God and His plan. He can take a bad incident and turn it into greater good. We didn't know if Nathaniel had been brain-damaged or would be seriously handicapped. God's plan might have included us ministering to other people as a result of this incident, perhaps for parents without faith who need someone to talk to.

My prayer was, "God, please make everything all right with Nathaniel. I want You to heal my son and make him healthy and normal. But if that is not Your plan and we are to be used in another way, I pray Your will be done."

Not too many years ago, I wouldn't have had the maturity to pray that way, because I was too selfish. God's not some great big wishing well in the sky. We have a give-and-take relationship: We learn what it is He wants for us and we accept His will. It's about being humble and letting go of your human desires and acknowledging that God's love for His children is powerful.

The first day when I went over to the intensive care unit, Nathaniel's breathing was raspy. You could hear the fluid in his lungs. He was still posturing with his arms, which wasn't a good sign. It was difficult, yet at the same time I had an increasing sense of calm and peace about the whole situation, a feeling that it was going to be okay. It was strange, because there was a very good chance that it wasn't going to be all right.

Some elders of our church came to the intensive care ward to pray. All the hospital staff knew they were there. I was confident God was hearing all our prayers and it was going to work out in the long run, even if the result was not what we wanted.

By the second day in intensive care, Nathaniel's seizures and posturing had decreased considerably. Then on the third day he had improved so much, I insisted that Janet's mother come over to see him. She had been almost as worried as we were.

After a week in intensive care at U.C.I.'s hospital, Nathaniel was brought back to our local hospital. The nurses commented that they had never seen such a dramatic improvement in a baby. In one week he had gone from "flatline," seizures and a dismal prognosis to being called a "miracle baby" by the pediatrician and the nurses.

Jesus said, "Believe I am in the Father and the Father is in me, and if you do not believe for my sake, believe for the sake of the miracles." Miracles are God's way of validating His son. People who would deny that there is any power in prayer have either never experienced it or they're just unwilling to turn to God.

JANET: Prayer is a heart-to-heart talk with God, my almighty Father. He protects me and is with me all the time. I don't pray to get physical or material things. I pray to get closer to God. God doesn't have to be reminded that we exist. We have to be reminded that *He* exists.

BOB: In prayer you open yourself to God communicating with you. Listening to God is as important as praying to Him. Jesus taught us how to pray. He gave us model prayers and commanded us to pray to God, to talk to God, and reminded us that God is good and there is a right and a wrong.

JANET: My spiritual path is improving. The more I learn, the better it gets. If you want to get good at something you have to work at it, so I try to read the Bible and pray every day.

The profound impact of my experience with Nathaniel will never wear off. How could it? You never think such a thing will happen to you. Then when it does, it gives you that much more faith. That's why God performs miracles. Even though He's no longer walking around in the form of Jesus healing people, He does heal. There are miracles.

Every day Bob and I realize how lucky we are. We could be visiting Nathaniel in an institution instead of having a normal, healthy baby at home with us. The doctors, the nurses and medicine played an important part in how well he's doing, but you certainly can't disregard God's hand in it. We have a beautiful son. Our prayers were answered.

BOB: There is not a day goes by that I don't look at Nathaniel and think, thank You, God, thank You.

THE BABY FROM HEAVEN

KELSEY TYLER

The sky over London, Ontario, was stormy gray that March 7 and the only sound in the Craenens' car was that of the wipers rhythmically clearing the windshield so John Craenen could see where he was going. Beside him, his wife Karen sat in silence, an occasional teardrop spilling onto her cheeks.

It was the darkest day of their lives. They had an hour before they would arrive at Victoria Hospital and Karen reflected on all that had brought them to this point.

She and John had married six years earlier and almost immediately began trying to have a baby. But months passed and still she was not pregnant.

"We could try fertility drugs," their doctor explained. "If they don't work, we could go with a number of other options."

The Craenens agreed but believed the situation would be simple to solve. There was no history of infertility in either family and they figured the medication would allow Karen to become pregnant almost immediately.

"Thank you for the medicine, and now, Lord, please let Karen conceive a child," John and Karen would sometimes pray. "I know You can hear me, Lord, and I look forward to Your answer."

But months passed and nothing happened, even after the doctor increased

Karen's level of medication. After three years, the doctor tried artificial insemination, but with no success. Finally, there remained only test tube fertilization, a procedure in which Karen's eggs and John's sperm were harvested from their bodies and fertilized in a test tube. The embryo was then implanted in Karen's uterus.

Three times the Craenens did this, but each time Karen miscarried.

About that time, Karen began complaining of sharp pain in her abdomen. The pain was occasional at first but then more constant and more severe. Finally her doctor diagnosed endometriosis, a painful condition that causes tissue to lodge in the ovaries and fallopian tubes.

"The only surefire cure is a hysterectomy," the doctor said at one of her appointments.

Karen shook her head, tears welling up in her eyes. "I want a baby, Doctor," she cried. "Not a hysterectomy."

The doctor sighed. "I understand. But endometriosis is very painful and it will only get worse with time. The chances of your getting pregnant are even slimmer than before, because of this condition. Just keep the hysterectomy in mind. It's one way to be sure you don't have to live with terrible pain all your life."

Karen left the office in tears and cried all the way home. She shared the news with John, who was crushed.

"I just don't understand," John said, shaking his head. "I've prayed about this so much, and you have, too. How come God won't let us have a baby?"

Karen shrugged sadly. "I guess we'll never really understand."

In the weeks that followed, Karen dealt with increasing pain of her endometriosis with a quiet faith, continuing to pray about the situation and to ask God for a child. But John grew angry with God, frustrated over the length of time he'd been praying about the situation with no apparent answer.

He was at work one day when a co-worker asked him about whether he and Karen were still trying to have a baby.

"Of course," he said, his voice tinged with anger. "We've wanted a baby for years."

The woman looked strangely at John. "You seem angry."

John uttered a short laugh. "Yeah, I guess you could say that."

"There's nothing to be mad about," she said gently. "Sometimes people can't have children. It's not like it's anyone's fault."

John studied the woman. "You don't understand," he said. "Karen and I have done our best to live a good, Christian life. We've asked God every day to be gracious and bring us a child. Instead, Karen's developed this endometriosis where she has sharp pain all through her abdomen."

"So you're angry at God?" John's co-worker asked simply.

John hesitated. "Yes. I guess I am. I'm mad at God because He isn't answering our prayers. Why should we have to go through this when all we want is a family like anyone else?"

The young woman was quiet a moment, and when she spoke, her voice was still quiet. "Why shouldn't you have to go through something painful?" she asked.

"Huh?"

"Why shouldn't you have to have this trial? Everywhere you look there are people suffering from a million different heartaches. God still cares about you. But this isn't Heaven. You can't think you should be exempt from having a little trouble down here."

John was taken aback by her brutal honesty. Suddenly he realized he had been presumptuous with God, expecting that he and Karen would be spared from the problems that occur daily in the lives of others, even other believers.

"Well, I gotta get back to work," she said as she shrugged and turned away.

"Hey, wait," John said. She turned back then and looked at John. "Thanks. I think I needed to hear that."

That night John shared the conversation with his wife.

"Maybe we should give the situation up to God and let him know that we trust Him, even if you never get pregnant."

Karen sighed. "Could you really do that, John? I mean, you won't be happy without a child."

John studied his wife. "Karen, I didn't marry you so you could be a baby machine. I married you because I love you. And if we never have children, then we are still a family. Maybe it's time we get on with life and start acting like one."

In the year that followed, the Craenens began taking more trips together and enjoying each other's company. They stopped searching for new pregnancy-inducing procedures and Karen quit taking fertility drugs.

"You're not mad at God anymore, are you?" she asked one day when they were vacationing in Acapulco.

"No, I'm at peace with Him. He knows I would still love to have a child, but if it never happens, then I'll always be thankful He gave me you." He kissed his wife. "And think of how much freedom we have compared to our friends who have kids."

Karen laughed. "That's true."

"No diapers, no burp rags, no baby-sitters."

Karen was laughing harder now. "Quit. Where's my husband? What did you do with him?"

John grinned. "Whatever God has planned for us is fine with me. I just want you to know I mean it."

In the next few months the pain from Karen's endometriosis grew worse than ever. Finally, she felt she had no choice but to schedule the hysterectomy.

"You could always adopt, Karen," the doctor said, empathetic to the fact that much of his patient's pain was emotional.

Karen looked at John and the couple nodded sadly. "We're not ready to talk about that yet. We still have to get through the hysterectomy."

The doctor understood. Many times women faced with an early hysterectomy needed time to grieve the loss of children they would never have. The Craenens' situation was particularly difficult since the doctor had been treating them for infertility for years and now would have to schedule a surgery that would forever end the couple's chance of having a child.

The surgery was set for March 7, and as the couple drove to the hospital that dark, stormy day they felt lower than at any point in their marriage.

"It'll be good to have you get rid of the pain," John said lamely, trying desperately to remain positive.

Karen nodded, not really listening. In her mind she was picturing children playing in their yard, a baby in her arms. Why, she wondered, couldn't she and John have a child of their own?

They arrived at the hospital on time and a surgical team was waiting. Karen was prepped for the operation and John squeezed her hand before leaving the room.

"We'll be okay," he said, as much for his benefit as hers. "God will get us through somehow."

Karen blinked back tears and nodded. "I love you."

"I love you, too. See you in a few hours."

John left for the waiting room and Karen was wheeled into surgery. They found what they expected to find—a bruised and battered uterus, ripe with scar tissue and disease. But they found something else, too.

A seven-month-old fetus, alive and kicking inside Karen's womb.

"This is impossible," one of the surgeons said, quickly stitching Karen back up. "Why didn't anyone check to see if she was pregnant?"

Karen's doctor was on staff at the hospital and he was summoned to the operating room. He explained that the medication she'd been taking for the endometriosis had also stopped her menstrual cycle.

"We've tried everything possible to get her pregnant and this past year she quit the fertility medication. I never would have guessed in a million years that she could get pregnant on her own, let alone without the help of medication and while suffering from endometriosis."

Karen was taken into a recovery room, and when the anesthesia wore off, she opened her eyes slowly and saw her doctor sitting nearby. He took her hand and smiled warmly.

"Karen I've got good news for you," he said. "You're expecting a baby."

Karen blinked hard, certain that she was still caught up in the effects of the medication. Then she looked and saw another woman in a bed near her.

"Doctor, you must have the wrong patient."

He shook his head and grinned again. "No. They went in to take out your uterus and they found a baby growing inside. You're seven months pregnant."

"And the baby's okay?" Karen began shaking and crying at the same time.

The doctor nodded. "He's fine. But we'll have to watch you really close because of the operation. There's a chance you could deliver earlier than normal."

Karen swallowed hard. "Someone get John. Please."

John was still waiting for word about the surgery when the doctor approached him. "Karen wants to see you," he said simply. "She has something to tell you."

Cancer, John thought instantly. *They got inside and found cancer in her uterus. She probably only has a few months to live.*

He stood up. Feeling a heavy weight in his heart, he followed the doctor to Karen's room. She looked up as he walked through the door. Instantly he could see she'd been crying. *Dear God, give me strength*, he prayed.

"Honey, you better sit down," she said.

"No, I don't want to sit down. Just tell me what's wrong."

Karen grinned then and shook her head. "Nothing's wrong, John. We're going to have a baby. I'm seven months pregnant."

John felt the floor fall away from him and he wondered if he might faint. Then suddenly he was crying as he reached across the hospital bed and took Karen in his arms.

"It's a miracle," he cried softly. "How can it be anything else?"

The doctor had been watching the scene and he stepped forward now and crossed his arms. His face was a mask of confusion.

"I can tell you that in all my years of medical experience neither I nor anyone on staff here has ever see anything like this," he said, pacing the room and then stopping to stare in awe at the couple. "She has the uterus of an eighty-year-old woman because of the scarring and endometriosis. Besides that she has a severe infertility problem." He shook his head in wonder. "Now we go to remove her uterus and find a healthy seven-month-old fetus. The medical community can say what it will about this but I guarantee you it's nothing short of a miracle."

Because of her high-risk condition, Karen was ordered to stay in bed for the remainder of her pregnancy. Several weeks after the attempted hysterectomy, blond, blue-eyed Brock was born at St. Joseph's Health Centre. He weighed just under four pounds and was kept in the hospital's neonatal intensive care unit until he gained a pound and then was sent home.

John and Karen carried the infant carefully to their waiting car and buckled him into his car seat.

"Before we go anywhere, I have some thanking to do," John said. He smiled at Karen and then looked tenderly at little Brock as he bowed his head. "Lord, a long time ago I stopped asking why we couldn't have a baby. I accepted that we might have trouble like anyone else. But now You've given us Brock when we never expected him to come along. He's a miracle baby, straight from You, and for as long as I live I will be thankful."

ADOPTING A DREAM

KATHRYN LAY

Michael or Michelle. Before Richard and I married, we agreed that this would be the name of our first child. We had it all planned.

Two years later, Richard walked across the stage to receive his college diploma. It was time to make our dream for a family come true.

For the next two years, we prayed that I would get pregnant, yet month after month was filled with disappointment. Then one day in the spring of 1985, I was so sure I was pregnant that I made an appointment to see the doctor.

With a smile, he said, "You're pregnant."

I wanted to dance around the room. My due date was set for the first week of November, "around the third," my doctor said.

The next six weeks were filled with preparations. We did everything but take out an ad in the newspaper. Richard began preparing the room that would be the nursery. We tried to imagine what our son or daughter would be like. My thoughts were consumed with the child growing inside me.

"I'm concerned that we haven't heard a heartbeat," my doctor told me on my third visit.

A half-hour later, I cried in his office when he explained that a blood test showed no sign of my ever having been pregnant.

"A false pregnancy," he said. "Your mind wanted it so badly, your body believed it."

Little Michael or Michelle didn't exist. There was no baby to mourn, yet we grieved.

So began nearly a decade of infertility tests and watching enviously as our friends and siblings had babies. My heart ached as I forced smiles when they talked of their children.

More pregnancy tests. More pacing and praying. Negative. They were always the same. The dream died again and again. We plunged into our work—Richard into his teaching and I into my writing. Yet our desire for a child was strong, and in 1992 we attended an adoption orientation class.

I looked around the crowded room of nervous couples. Could our dream really come true?

I was afraid to hope.

"This is our chance," Richard whispered.

We began our required parenting classes. Every Monday evening for ten weeks we listened, role-played and discussed the joy and trials of parenting these children who needed new homes.

With all the work came the joy of preparation. How long before our child arrived? Would he or she come with a broken heart and spirit? How long would it take to bond with our child, and he with us? Would our child be anything like the one I'd imagined so long ago?

Together Richard and I prepared our extra bedroom. Would it be a nursery or child's room? There were so many plans to make, yet so little information to help us. Lovingly I placed bottles of lotion and powders beside bibs and books, inside dresser drawers.

Often, I sat on the floor in the yellow and white room and dreamed of the child who would sleep and play there. I bought a few toys and stuffed animals. They waited quietly for small hands to hold them.

Then, on November 3, 1993, the phone rang and our lives changed.

"Kathy, is there something you've been wanting for Christmas?" our caseworker asked.

I could almost hear her smiling. I clutched the phone and whispered, "Yes."

"Well, we've got some good news."

Then she told me about an eight-month-old girl. A baby girl! Would I awake and find it just another dream?

"Her name is Theresa Michelle. But her foster parents call her Michelle," I was told.

I was stunned. Michelle. Eight years ago, we'd dreamed of our Michelle. Then it hit me. It was November 3. If I had had that child in November of 1985, "around the third," my doctor had said, he or she would be eight years old. How wonderful God was to us, how our prayers had been answered!

I tried to imagine what it would be like holding this child.

Within two weeks, we began our three days of visitation. I looked into my daughter's face. She smiled and held her arms out. I held her and breathed in the scent of baby powder and milk, as sweet-smelling as a garden of roses.

Our Michelle had arrived.

On November 23, she came to live in our home and hearts. Every day our love for her grows. Nearly four years old now, she loves to hear the story of her adoption, of how we waited and longed for her.

Hopes and dreams don't have to die. We watched ours come back to life and call us Mama and Daddy.

THE EARTHMOVER

LES BROWN

Child choking! . . . Handle Code Three!" Dreaded words. I responded immediately, flipping on red lights and siren as the dispatcher gave the address and directions. *Just my luck,* I thought as I sped past parked cars and passed drivers who did not pull over on the highway.

I had just begun my working day. Actually it was my day off, and I had been called in to cover for another officer who was ill. I knew next to nothing about this particular beat in Los Angeles and intended to drive around it to familiarize myself with the area. Now, my first call was a life-and-death emergency several miles away.

I had been a patrol officer for some time, but no matter how many life-and-death situations an officer faces, when a child is involved the heart beats a little faster, the foot is a little heavier on the accelerator, the urgency is greater.

I decided to take the unfinished freeway; it was next to impossible to get through the traffic on Highway 101. Just ahead was the street that would take me to my destination. Then, anguish swept through me. *There was no off-ramp.* Between me and that road was a deep, wide ditch and a steep embankment.

Tires screeched as I stopped, red lights still flashing. I got out and looked down at the busy road so far below me.

God help me! I cried out silently. *What am I going to do? If I go around I'll be too late.*

"What's the matter, Officer?"

I looked up, and saw a man sitting on top of the biggest earth-moving vehicle I have ever seen. He must have been sitting two stories high.

"Child choking to death . . . I have to get down there," I gestured blindly, "but there's no road. If I go around I'll never make it."

Years of discipline had taught me to control my emotions, but I was in an agony of frustration.

"Follow me, Officer—*I'll make you a road!*"

I jumped in my car and took off after him, amazed at what the mammoth machine could do. The huge buckets on the side of it were full of dirt. He dumped them into the ditch.

The clock had become my enemy.

Hurry! Hurry! Hurry!

The earthmover started down the long sloping embankment, scattering dirt. Huge clouds of dust enveloped us. It seemed like hours, but in reality it was a short time before the earthmover lumbered down on the highway, blocking traffic in both directions.

Hurry!

I raced, siren screaming, the few short blocks to the street I had been given, and frantically searched for the correct address. Almost at once I found it.

As I burst through the doorway, a terrified young mother handed me her tiny baby boy. I could see she was going to be no help. The baby was already blue. Was I too late?

"God . . . help."

All I remember about the next few seconds was turning the baby upside down, smacking his back. The deadly object flew from his throat onto the floor. It was a button that had let a tiny bit of air through, but not enough.

I was aware of another siren.

A fireman rushed into the room.

Precious oxygen.

The child screamed, turned red, flailing his tiny fists. He was angry, but very much alive.

Back in my car I logged the incident, reported in by radio and drove down the street, shaken, but elated.

I glanced up at the sky. "Thank You."

This, then, was what it was all about. Lately I had found myself wondering if this kind of life was really worthwhile. The hostility, the criminals, the dregs of society. The petty little things that took time and energy to deal with. A thankless job. Was this the life I wanted?

Yet, with God's help, we had just saved a baby's life. And, in this act, my own life had suddenly come into perspective. That little mite in distress had taught me that I had important work to do and that I would be helped in this work by a loving, caring God who would hear a prayer and help a troubled cop get his car over a ditch.

Another call came. Then another, and so on through the day.

The next day I was determined to learn the patrol area before anything else happened. I never wanted to get caught like that again. As I drove along I approached the place where I had stood in desperation twenty-four hours before. I slowed as I again saw the gigantic earthmover. I wanted to thank him. The driver waved and yelled.

As he ran toward me, I could see he was deeply moved. He stammered, "The . . . the baby . . ." He stopped, unable to speak.

Surprised at his deep emotion, I tried to reassure him, "The baby is all right. Thanks to you—you helped save his life. I never would have made it in time. Man, that was teamwork."

He gulped, "I . . . I know . . . but what I didn't know when . . . when I helped you was . . ." He bit his lip hard, then added in a whisper, "That was my son."

Chapter 6   God's Lessons Last a Lifetime

When we first meet David, he is just a boy, a shepherd caring for his father's flocks. This youngest son of Jesse seems to have spent a lot of time away from home tending sheep. He passed the time writing music, honing his weapons skills, fighting off predators—skills that would come to serve him well all through his life.

We know more about David than probably anyone else in the Old Testament, since we read not only the accounts of his life and his exploits, but also his own words in his poetry. We see David's life in its entirety, not simply in episodes, and we view David as a multidimensional person, not only in profile.

His young life is filled with adventures and drama. He's only a boy when he's anointed by Samuel as the king who will succeed Saul, and he's still a boy when he challenges Goliath. Most of what David knew about God's love and character was learned when he was just a boy.

What becomes apparent about this remarkable character is that his relationship with God that began as a boy shepherd lasts his whole life, always growing, developing, deepening. The insights and truth learned as a boy became a foundation for a relationship that lasted a lifetime. Just as the melodies composed on Judean hillsides were transformed into the comforting words of Psalm 23, so a rough and tumble boy was transformed into a godly king who ruled a nation.

The lessons we learn as children are woven into the fabric of our character, allowing us to carry with us always the miraculous ways that God touches our lives. May we always remember God's lessons learned in childhood.

> For you have been my hope, O Sovereign LORD,
>   my confidence since my youth.
>   From birth I have relied on you;
> you brought me forth from my mother's womb.
>   I will ever praise you. . . .
>   But as for me, I will always have hope. . . .
> Since my youth, O God, you have taught me,
> and to this day I declare your marvelous deeds.
>   Even when I am old and gray,
>   do not forsake me, O God,
> till I declare your power to the next generation,
>   your might to all who are to come.
>
> —Psalm 71:5–6, 14, 17–18

CUP FULL OF WATER

CLARA WALLACE NAIL

When we were newlyweds, my husband Edwin announced one day that we needed to move back to his family's farm. He said he had to help his dad run the place, which I could accept. What I couldn't accept is that we would be leaving the little house I loved on my own family's property.

I wouldn't be able to run up the path through the woods to Aunt Berta's every time I needed something or wanted to visit. I would miss the soothing view of the pasture as I looked out the window. Most of all I hated to leave the beautiful bed of zinnias I had just planted.

Tears fell on the old newspaper I used to wrap dishes before packing them for the move. Curtains were rolled up, the beds stripped and taken apart. I was so sad about dismantling our house, I couldn't think of my young husband and how he must have felt, giving up a job he liked to take on acres and acres of cotton and grain, not to mention a herd of cows.

Because I had to, I made the move. We painted some of the inside of the ugly house that was now ours, but there was no money to do anything else. Edwin was gone all day in the field, so I had a lot of time to rattle around by myself. The more I looked at the old place, the more discouraged I became. It was impossible to heat, impossible to make comfortable. There just wasn't anything to be done.

Feeling disgusted, I went outside to work in the garden. The sun was warm and the rosebushes needed attention. I thought some mulch would be good for them, so I got the cart and went off to the pine grove.

I always feel worshipful in a pine grove. The sun filtering through the towering trees, the sweet resiny scent of pine, the silence—it's like a sanctuary. While kneeling on a cushion of pine needles I found myself talking to God: "I'm sorry for the bitterness in me, Lord. Please take it away and give me peace." I stopped and listened for a while. But all that came to me was the whisper of the trees as they moved in the breeze. I returned to my work.

After forking pine straw into the car, I realized I was thirsty. Rather than go back to the drafty house I walked down the hill a few feet to the creek where a cold spring ran out of the bank. Kneeling at the water's edge, I bent forward and cupped my hands. As the clear, cold water flowed into them a forgotten scene flowed into my memory.

On a faraway afternoon when I was a child, my hand was holding Daddy's as we walked across the lawn, the sun beaming down on us. "Daddy," I said, "I'm thirsty."

He chuckled. "Well, then, we must get you a drink."

We stopped at a rusty old spigot sticking out of the ground. I watched him kneel and turn the water on to a slow trickle. Bewildered, I pointed out, "But, Daddy, there's no cup."

His face crinkled into a smile. "Then we'll use what we have," he said.

He brought my hands together, showing me how to cup them, the fingers pressed tightly together so the water would form a little pool. I put my lips at the edge and drank.

Now as I knelt by the spring, recalling the scene, the bitterness washed from me and the despair was gone. We'll use what we have. Daddy had been right. God expects us to work at making the best of what we are given. I could continue to make myself miserable, or I could use what I had to make our home and my life more pleasant.

I wheeled the cart of pine straw back to the house, ideas whirling in my head. I could set Great-grandmother's soup tureen on the old washstand we had refinished and put candlesticks on each side. I could trim the green drapes, and make some bright cushion covers from the scraps. It wouldn't exactly be ready for a decorating magazine, but it would be home.

There we welcomed our firstborn, and the next year we moved to our own farm. The first thing I did was to find a spring at the creek. On a hot day when our son was young we walked down to it and knelt beside the cool, clear water for a drink. "Cup your hands," I told him. "We'll use what we have."

PICTURE PERFECT

HOPE GARDNER

The baby's scream from the bathroom stopped my heart. I raced in, horrified to think what I might find. My six-year-old Amy, who was trying to be extra helpful to me during my uncomfortable pregnancy, had decided that she would bathe my toddler. I had asked her to turn on the bathwater, but she decided to take it a little further. She filled the tub about three inches deep just as she had seen me do many times, took Shaun's clothes off and gently put him in the tub. When I reached him, he was standing in three inches of scalding hot water. Amy had inadvertently turned on just the hot tap, and Shaun's tiny feet were being burned.

I grabbed him, threw him into the sink, and instantly turned on the cold water to stop the burning. In a moment of panic and anger, I turned to Amy and said, "How could you do this? Look how badly you've burned his feet!" Amy ran from the bathroom in tears, and for the next ten minutes, I took care of Shaun's little feet. When I realized he was all right and the burn wasn't as bad as I had thought at first, I went looking for Amy. She was nowhere to be found until finally I heard her whimpers coming from underneath her bed. Amy's tender feelings had been injured more seriously than her brother's feet, and I felt terrible.

As I tried to coax her out from under the bed, I begged for her forgiveness. I tried to explain that I hadn't meant what I had said and that I had been reacting out of fear. No matter how hard I tried, she would not come out from hiding. Since I was seven months pregnant, even getting down on the floor took some negotiating; crawling under the bed to pull her out was out of the question. So I stretched my arm as far as it would go to try and reach her. Just as my hand brushed against her, she jerked her head, and somehow a prong on my wedding ring scratched her face. When she cried out and grabbed her cheek, I thought my heart would break.

She finally crawled out, and I saw what I had done. It was horrible—the scratch was about three inches long, and even though it wasn't deep, it was red and swollen and bleeding. I grabbed an ice pack and held her in my arms, both of us weeping now. I was furious at myself for hurting not only Amy's feelings but also her pretty face. To make the situation even worse, I remembered that the next day at school was "picture day" and Amy had been looking forward to it for days. Now her adorable smile would be overshadowed by a big, red, swollen scratch.

When she awoke the next morning the scratch was still obvious. I iced it one more time and sent her on her way. I waited nervously over the next few weeks. Even though Amy had seemingly forgotten the incident, I was still bothered by it and dreaded seeing the picture. Even though I hadn't intended to scratch her, I knew the picture would serve as a constant reminder of my angry words that had precipitated the accident and left such an indelible mark on her spirit. I had hurt my most precious possession—my child—and felt very sad whenever I thought about it.

And then the day came when Amy rushed in from school holding her picture packet tightly in her hand. I knew she was excited, but I opened the envelope slowly, wanting to postpone the inevitable. What happened in the next instant was something for which I have no explanation; it was a miracle of the purest form. For there on Amy's school picture was a little girl with a beautiful smile and creamy, flawless skin. I examined it over and over—there was no mark of any kind on her face. It was simply gone.

We had told no one of the incident. We knew the photographer hadn't removed it—with the thousands of schoolchildren photographed, touch-ups were never part of the package. But there she was—my precious daughter—happy, perfect, beautiful, as if nothing had ever happened the night before. Now, twenty years later, the eight-by-ten copy of that picture still hangs in our home, a treasure to my heart.

Motherhood is the most demanding and emotionally taxing thing I've ever done. Like most mothers, I often become exhausted and frustrated and occasionally do or say things I later regret. I don't know who provided the sweet miracle that day the picture came home, but for all the years since, it has been a symbol of the fact that someone is watching out for mothers, making the road a little smoother when we occasionally come to the end of our rope. And as I continue to struggle through the everyday challenges of motherhood, it serves as a gentle reminder to look heavenward for the example of a perfect parent who loves with a perfect love.

THE DAY HEALING BEGAN

Marilyn K. Strube

Snow crunched angrily under my tires, and my car's headlights made only feeble streaks through the driving snow. My eyes ached from trying to find my way through an unfamiliar neighborhood.

As a certified medical assistant, I was making a house call to administer a flu shot to an elderly, bedridden patient. When the request had come into the doctor's office, there had been so much red tape concerning the vaccination that I finally volunteered to do it myself. I was frustrated then at all the fuss and bother; now I was angry at myself for getting involved.

I know all about frustration. One week earlier, the trial of my sixteen-year-old daughter's attacker finally ended. She had been kidnapped and raped by a stranger. He had been sentenced to five and a half years. *Not long enough*, I thought bitterly.

Later that day, as I relayed the judge's ruling to my mother, she asked what I thought would have been fair. I didn't know. I only knew I wanted to sleep through the night without nightmares. I wanted the tension between my husband Joe and me to be over. I didn't want to be afraid to let my children walk to school.

I glanced at the clock on the dashboard. Seven o'clock. Usually by this time, I would be in pajamas and on my second glass of wine. Without alcohol to deaden my senses, scenes from the courtroom would come, unbidden, to mind. Erica's lawyer questioning the rapist, "Which part of 'No!' didn't you understand?" And then Erica on the witness stand being asked to "describe in detail what he did to you." The windshield wipers reminded me of Erica swiping at tears as she recalled the atrocities.

I pulled up in front of the house and took a deep breath to release my tension and anger. Would I ever feel normal again? Just then, the house's front door opened and a little girl in the doorway yelled back over her shoulder. "She's here!"

Dogs barked in the background. I didn't feel like dealing with yowling dogs and a little girl in addition to an elderly patient. I wanted to give the shot and go home. A woman appeared and pushed the two dogs back so I could enter.

"Hi Marilyn," she greeted me. "I'm Judy, and this is my granddaughter, Gwynney. Thanks for coming! Can I get you something to eat or drink?"

"No, thanks. I've got to get home and make dinner for my family," I lied. I knew Joe would have fed the children by now.

Then Gwynney peeked from behind her grandmother's legs. She was a chubby little thing with a mop of blond hair. When I looked at her closely, I shivered. Gwynney was almost my daughter's double when Erica was the same age.

"We just made macaroni and cheese," the child volunteered. "You can take it home to your 'fambly' if you want."

The telephone rang. "Gwynney," Judy instructed, "show Marilyn to Great-Grandma's room while I get the phone."

Gwynney nodded, taking her responsibility seriously. "I'm five years old," she informed me.

"No, you're not!" Judy called from the kitchen. "She's only three, Marilyn."

Gwynney smiled sheepishly then pointed to the bigger dog, a dignified yellow Labrador with a graying muzzle. "This is Barney," she said. Barney thumped his tail politely. Pointing to the other dog, a mixed German shepherd with intelligent eyes, she said, "And this is Susie." Susie woofed. "Okay," Gwynney concluded, "now I will take you to Great-Grandma's room."

I put my coat on the living room couch and fell in behind Gwynney and the dogs. Judy reappeared just as we entered the old woman's bedroom. "Mom," she yelled in her mother's ear, "the nurse is going to give you a shot!" When there was no response, Judy pushed back her mother's hair and kissed her gently on the forehead.

"I'll be in the other room if you need me," she said, and quietly left the room.

I loaded the syringe and was about to give the injection when I looked over my shoulder. Gwynney, Barney and Susie were lined up in order of size against the wall. Each was watching my every move.

I stopped and explained what I was doing. "Don't worry," I reassured them, "this won't hurt your great-grandma."

Gwynney nodded. As I turned, I heard her reassuring the dogs, "this won't hurt Great-Grandma, so don't worry."

Six months before, I would have smiled. Now I just swabbed the woman's arm with alcohol and administered the shot.

The moment I withdrew the needle, Gwynney was at my side with a wastebasket to collect my disposable gloves. "Boy, you really have the program down, don't you?" I said, laughing in spite of myself.

Gwynney looked at me seriously. "Are you sad?" she asked.

"What makes you ask?" I stammered, taken aback.

"Well, your laugh sounds kind of sad."

I knelt and gave her a hug. "You sure are smart for a three-year-old," I said, tousling her fine golden hair. "You could pass for a five-year-old any day."

Gwynney bolted for the kitchen. There, I heard her telling her grandmother, "She says I could pass for a five-year-old!"

After Judy thanked me profusely for coming, Gwynney and the dogs walked me to the door. "I hope you feel happy soon," she said and squeezed my hand.

"Thank you," I answered. "Me, too."

Gwynney waved, and the dogs wagged their tails as I left. Outside, the storm had passed. It had turned colder, and snow squeaked under my feet as I made my way to the car. The dark sky was full of stars. I started the car but didn't go half a block before I had to pull over by the curb.

Tears flooded out of me, as I cried out, "God, why didn't you protect Erica?" All the feelings I had squelched over the past six months poured out. I let God have it with both barrels.

First, tears of bitterness. And then sadness, the sadness that was so obvious to Gwynney. I grieved for my daughter's stolen innocence. I was sad that with all Joe and I were able to provide, we weren't able to keep her safe.

Then a stillness enveloped my car, and I fell silent. I thought of all the things that had happened to us in the past six months. I remembered the faces of the homeless that we passed each day driving to court, and the battered women and children who lined the corridors as we made our way into the courtroom. Until six months before, I had known only the safe haven that had been our world. Our family had been so richly blessed.

Suddenly, I was thanking God for all the goodness in our lives. "Lord," I said, "I need to move beyond this and start living again. You've given me so much. Help me to focus on those who really need Your help."

Tomorrow, I vowed, I would not retreat into pajamas and wine. Instead, I would go home and make my "fambly" macaroni and cheese. I would smile more and offer words of encouragement. I would brighten the world around me.

Peace washed over me. I forgave myself for not being there to shield Erica from harm.

I looked back at Gwynney's house, where the porch light still glowed warmly into the night. I smiled.

"Lord, thank You for Gwynney," I prayed. "Her resemblance to Erica and her wise words melted my heart."

HEART SOUNDS

TIM MADIGAN

One afternoon about a week before Christmas, my family of four piled into our minivan to run a short errand, and this question came from a small voice in the back seat: "Dad," began my five-year-old son Patrick, "how come I've never seen you cry?"

Just like that. No preamble. No warning. One minute it's, "Mom, what's for supper?" The next it's, "Dad, how come . . ." My wife Catherine was as surprised by this as I was. But she is one of those lucky souls for whom tears come naturally—spilled spontaneously then quickly forgotten. Patrick has seen his mother cry dozens of times, so my wife was entitled to turn my way in the front passenger seat with a mischievous smile that said, "Explain this one, Dad." I couldn't, of course. I mumbled something in reply about crying when my son was not around, at sad movies and so forth. But I knew immediately that Patrick had put his finger on the largest obstacle to my own peace and contentment, the dragon-filled moat separating me from the fullest human expression of joy, anger and disappointment. Simply put, I could not cry.

I know I am scarcely the only man for whom this is true. In fact I believe that tearless men are the rule in our society, not the exception. When, for instance, did John Wayne shed tears, or Kirk Douglas, or any of those other Hollywood archetypes of manliness? When Wayne's best buddy had been slain on the battlefield, the Duke looked down to the body of his fallen friend with studied sobriety, but also with his typical calm. Then he moved on to the next battle with his typical bravado.

We men. We fathers and sons have been condemned to follow Wayne's lead. Passing centuries have conditioned us to believe that stoicism is the embodiment of strength and unfettered emotion that of weakness. We have feigned imperviousness to the inevitable slings and arrows, traveling through life with stiff upper lips, calm on the outside, secretly dying within.

A recent television news report only confirmed what I have long suspected. According to the news, the number of men being diagnosed with depression today is skyrocketing. But I submit that we men have always been depressed to one degree or another, though we tend to medicate it with alcohol, or work, or afternoons and evenings sitting mindlessly in front of one televised sports event or another.

Take me, for instance. For most of my adult life I have battled chronic depression, an awful and insidious disorder that saps life of its color and meaning, and too often leads to self-destruction. Doctors have said much of my problem is physiological, an inherited chemical imbalance, something akin to diabetes. Those physicians have treated it as such with medication.

But I also know that much of my illness is attributable to years of swallowing my rage, my sadness, even my joy. Strange as it seems, in this world, where macho is everything, drunkenness and depression are safer ways for men like me to deal with feelings than tears.

In my own battle, I had begun to see the folly of this long ago, well before my son's penetrating backseat query. I could only hope the same debilitating handicap would not be passed on to the generation that followed mine.

Hence our brief conversation on the sunny December afternoon after Patrick's question. He and I were back in the van after playing together at a park near our home. Before pulling out, I turned to my son and thanked him for his curiosity of the day before. Tears were a very good thing for boys and girls alike, I said. Crying is God's way of healing people when they are sad.

"I'm very glad you can cry whenever you're sad or whenever you're angry." I said. "Sometimes daddies have a harder time showing how they feel. You know, Patrick, I wish I were more like you in that way. Someday I hope to do better."

Patrick nodded. But in truth, I held out little hope. Lifelong habits are hard to break. I was sure it would take something on the order of a miracle for me to connect with the dusty core of my own emotions.

From the time he was an infant, my son has enjoyed an unusual passion and affinity for music. By age four, he could pound out several bars of Wagner's

Ride of the Valkyries by ear on the piano. More recently, he had spent countless hours singing along with the soundtrack to the *Hunchback of Notre Dame,* happily directing the music during the most orchestral parts. But these were hidden pleasures for him, enjoyed in the privacy of his own room or with the small and forgiving audience of his mother, father and older sister, Melanie.

What the youth director of our church suggested was something different altogether.

"I was wondering if Patrick would sing a verse of 'Away in the Manger' during the early service on Christmas Eve," Juli Bail, the youth director, asked on our telephone answering machine.

My son's first solo. My wife and I struggled to contain our excitement and anxiety. Catherine delicately broached the possibility, gently prodding Patrick after Juli's call, reminding him how beautifully he sang, telling him how much fun it would be. Patrick himself seemed less convinced. His face crinkled into a frown.

"You know, Mom," he said, "sometimes when I have to do something important, I get kind of scared."

Grown-ups feel that way, too, he was quickly assured, but the decision to sing on Christmas Eve was left to him. Should Patrick choose to postpone his singing debut, that would be fine with his parents. His deliberations took only a few minutes.

"Okay," Patrick said. "I'll do it."

For the next week, Patrick practiced his stanza several times with his mother. A formal rehearsal at the church had also gone extremely well, my wife reported. But I could only envision myself at age five, singing into a microphone before hundreds of people. When Christmas Eve arrived, my expectations of my son's performance were limited indeed.

My son's solo came late in the service. By then, the spirit of the evening and many beautiful performances by young voices had served to thaw my inner reaches, like a Minnesota snow bank on a sunny day in March.

Then Patrick and his young choir took the stage. Catherine, Melanie and I sat with the congregation in darkness as a spotlight found my son, standing alone at the microphone. He was dressed in white and wore a pair of angel wings, and he sang that night as if he had done so forever. Patrick hit every note, slowly, confidently, and those few moments, as his five-year-old voice washed over the people, he seemed transformed, a true angel, bestower of Christmas miracles. There was eternity in Patrick's voice that night, penetrating beauty rich enough to dissolve centuries of manly reserve.

At the sound of my son, heavy tears welled at the corners of my eyes, and spilled down my cheeks.

His song was soon over and the congregation applauded. Catherine brushed away tears. Melanie, my daughter, sobbed next to me. Others wept, too. After the service, I moved quickly to congratulate Patrick, but found he had more urgent priorities. "Mom," he said as his costume was stripped away, "I really have to go to the bathroom."

So Patrick disappeared. As he did, my friend and pastor, Dick Lord, wished me a Merry Christmas. But emotion choked off my reply as the two of us embraced. Outside the sanctuary in our crowded gathering place, I received congratulations from fellow church members. But I had no time to bask there in Patrick's reflected glory. I knew I had only a short window in which to act, only a few minutes before my natural stoicism closed around my heart. I found my son as he emerged from the church bathroom.

"Patrick, I need to talk to you about something." I said, sniffling.

Alarm crossed his face. "Is it something bad?" he asked.

"No, it's not something bad." I answered.

"Is it something good?"

I took him by the hand and led him down the long hallway, into a darkened room where we could be alone. I knelt to his height and admired his young face in the shadows, the large blue eyes, the dusting of freckles on his nose and cheeks, the dimples on one side.

He looked at my moist eyes quizzically, with concern.

"Patrick, do you remember when you asked me why you had never seen me cry?" I began.

He nodded again.

"Why are you crying, Dad?'

"Your singing was so pretty it made me cry."

Patrick smiled proudly and flew into my arms. I began to sob.

"Sometimes," my son said into my shoulder, "life is just so beautiful you have to cry."

Our moment together was over too soon, for it was Christmas Eve, and untold treasures awaited our five-year-old beneath the tree at home. But I wasn't ready for the traditional plunge into Christmas giving just yet. I handed my wife the keys to the van and set off alone for the mile-long hike from our church to our home.

The night was cold and crisp. I crossed a small park and admired the full moon hanging low over a neighborhood brightly lit in the colors of the season. As I left the park and turned up a street toward home, I met a car moving slowly down the street, a family taking in the area's Christmas lights. Someone inside rolled down a backseat window.

"Merry Christmas," a child's voice yelled out to me.

"Merry Christmas," I yelled back, and the tears began to flow once again.

JUST MAKE ROOM

MARION BOND WEST

When I was raising four kids and my life was unbelievably harried, I still managed to connect with God daily amid all the chaos of motherhood. Twenty-something years later my life is quieter, even serene at times. I don't go around the house snatching up dirty laundry on the fly. The beds are always made. No children bellow "Mama!" every few minutes. They're all grown and have homes and children of their own.

I had always assumed when I entered this stage of my life I would relish spending more quality time with the Lord. Recently, though, I had found myself longing for those topsy-turvy days when finding a moment for God on a catch-as-catch-can basis brought an intensity to the encounters.

Back then, after the children were off to school and I was still in my bathrobe, between finishing the breakfast dishes and starting the laundry, I sat at the cluttered kitchen table for my quiet time. On Thursdays I usually took my Bible to the beauty shop and read while I sat under a hot, noisy dryer. While scrubbing the bathroom floors or hunched over my ironing board I talked with God effortlessly, as if He were a neighbor dropping by for a visit. Now when I sought Him I stalked around the neat, empty house like a skittish cat trying to find a place to nestle down.

One day I stood staring out the window at the new backyard gazebo my husband Gene had given me for my birthday, mulling over my sense of spiritual disconnect-edness. *Lord, are You and I drifting apart?* I wondered.

Just then I saw my youngest daughter Jennifer drive up with three-and-a-half-year-old Libby, who was going to spend the night with us. Jen was in a hurry, so she let Libby out with her hot-pink overnight bag. I went outside to the driveway and we waved good-bye to my daughter as she drove off.

"Hey, Nanny!" Libby said, her eyes growing big at the sight of the gazebo. "What's that? A playhouse?"

I laughed and pulled her close as we strolled across the yard. "It's called a gazebo. I've wanted one since I was your age. The man came to paint it yesterday."

"Is the paint dry?"

"Let's see." I touched a post. "Dry."

"Can we go in, Nanny?"

"I don't see why not."

I took her hand. We stepped inside, sat on the wooden glider and began to swing. Libby's little legs stuck straight out. "Wheeeeee...." Libby's honeyed ponytail lifted in the breeze. "This is fun!" she cried.

A few minutes she said in an excited voice, "Nanny, let's ask Jesus to come in here with us, okay?"

I slowed the glider, not quite sure how to respond. "All right, Libby," I finally said.

"Well," she directed, "move over and make a place. He can't come if you don't make room for Him."

I slid over obediently, staring at the space between my granddaughter and me.

"Good," Libby said. Then she sang, "Praise him, praise him, all ye little children . . ." she shot me a stern glance. "Sing, Nanny!"

I sang.

"God is love . . ."

All at once I felt it. The presence of God, unmistakable as the smell of fresh paint. We swung for a while until Libby said she was hungry, so we went inside to make supper. Later, after I put Libby to bed and read her a story, I went back outside. The fat July moon made it almost as bright as day. I stepped into the gazebo, sat down on the glider and stared at the shadow-striped space next to me. "Lord," I whispered, "please come and visit with me again. I welcome You here, and in every inch of my home and my heart."

I began to swing gently, savoring a blissful sense of spiritual relief. When I was a busy mother I had to take the simple step of inviting God in. But without those hectic rhythms of motherhood, I had stopped having to make room and floundered spiritually, thinking God would be there automatically. I had taken His presence for granted. But my granddaughter had reminded me about an important step I was forgetting.

I stuck my legs out, threw my head back in the moonlight and made room for the Lord.

www.guidepostsbooks.com
Guideposts Book & Inspirational Media Division
Series Editor: Patricia S. Klein
Designed by Monica Elias
Jacket photo courtesy of Photodisc
Typeset by Composition Technologies, Inc.
Typists: Rachel Eden, Jan Arroyo and Judith Silvio
Printed in the United States of America

This original Guideposts Book was created by the Book and Inspirational Media Division of the company that publishes *Guideposts*, a monthly magazine filled with true stories of hope and inspiration.

Guideposts is available by subscription. All you have to do is write to Guideposts, 39 Seminary Hill Road, Carmel, New York 10512. When you subscribe, each month you can count on receiving exciting new evidence of God's presence, His guidance and His limitless love for all of us.

Guideposts Books are available on the World Wide Web at www.guidepostsbooks.com. Follow our popular book of devotionals, *Daily Guideposts*, and read excerpts from some of our best-selling books. You can also send prayer requests to our Monday morning Prayer Fellowship and read stories from recent issues of our magazines, *Guideposts*, *Angels on Earth*, and *Guideposts for Teens*.